Don't get in a pickle over starting a career in law...

The Gherkin Guide to Securing a Training Contract

By Gherkin Guides

September 2007

This Guide is Copyright Protected

The views expressed within this book do not necessarily represent the views of all law firms. The book is intended as a general guide only. Its application to specific situations will depend on the particular circumstances involved and so should not be relied upon as a substitute for carrying out your own detailed research. Gherkin Guides and its authors do not accept responsibility for any errors it may contain or for any loss sustained by any person placing reliance on its contents.

Published by Gherkin Guides.

www.GherkinLaw.com

Don't get in a pickle over starting a career in law...

Introduction

Welcome to the Gherkin Guide to Securing a Training Contract.

About us

We are two trainee Solicitors that have undertaken our training contracts at a Magic Circle firm and mid-sized niche firm respectively. Between us we have completed 5 vacation schemes, attended countless open days and were fortunate enough to be offered a number of training contracts.

5 years ago, when we were going through the stressful application process, we wished for an independent, user-friendly, simple and practical guide to help us through the process.

Such a guide did not exist then and has not existed until now!

We have created the Gherkin Guide to pass on all the invaluable information we have learnt (from experience) about the entire trainee recruitment process, because we KNOW what it is like, what firms *really* want and, most importantly, how to succeed.

If you are looking for that **competitive edge**, read on...

www.GherkinLaw.com

Contents

SECTION 1:

THE ROUTE TO QUALIFICATION

The Route to Qualification Overview

There are several routes to qualifying as a Solicitor in England and Wales, but the two most common methods are outlined below...

The law degree route

1. Complete a law degree

There are many different law courses available at universities. In addition to the conventional 3-year law degree, there are many combined courses where it is possible to mix law with another subject such as a language or a year studying law abroad.

To be exempt from having to complete the Graduate Diploma in Law (GDL/CPE), your law or law-combined course must cover the following seven core subject areas:

- Contract
- Tort
- Criminal
- EU law
- Constitutional and Administrative law
- Land
- Equity and Trusts

2. Legal Practice Course (LPC)

This is a 1-year full-time course (it can also be carried out part-time). During the LPC you will study and be assessed on a number of different areas:

a. **Compulsory areas:** (Business Law and Practice, Property Law and Practice, and Civil and Criminal Litigation);

b. **Pervasive areas:** (Accounts, Professional Conduct and Client Care, European Union Law, Probate and Administrative, Revenue Law and Human Rights);

c. **Skills areas:** (Advocacy, Interviewing and Advising, Practical Legal Research, Writing and Drafting); and

d. **Elective subjects:** (Check that any particular subjects that you wish to study as electives are offered by the institutions you are applying to).

3. Training Contract

The Law Society requires that Solicitors complete a minimum of 2 years in a recognised (Law Society registered) law firm. As such, training contracts are generally completed over 2 years (possible time exemptions are available in some firms for those that have been a paralegal for 6 months or more). See page 161 for a more detailed explanation of what to expect during a training contract.

Following the successful completion of these 2 years working with a law firm and the requisite professional skills course (see page 162) you will be admitted to the official Roll of Solicitors.

The non-law degree route

1. Degree in any subject

Law firms recruit a large number of non-law graduates every year. They do not discriminate between Arts and Science subjects, and welcome the breadth of experience non-law graduates can bring to the workplace.

If you are unsure as to whether or not you are exempt from being required to complete the GDL/CPE, contact the Law society (www.lawsociety.org.uk).

2. Graduate Diploma in Law/ Common Professional Exams (GDL/CPE)

This is a 1-year full-time course (it can be carried out part-time) and covers the 7 core subject areas of a law degree. See page 155 for details and additional advice for non-law graduates.

3. Legal Practice Course (LPC) (see above)

4. Training Contract (see above)

Law Firms
Which one do I pick?

There are hundreds of law firms to choose from. We advise that you focus your applications carefully and avoid the scatter gun approach of applying to every law firm that you can think of! Your applications are unlikely to be specific or polished enough to impress. Decide what type of firm you would like to work for and which firm(s) you are best suited to. There is no point applying to a large commercial City firm if your dream is to specialise in Criminal or Human Rights law, so it is worth doing your research thoroughly.

Here is a very rough guide[1] to help...

Broad category	Example law firms	Description
"Magic Circle"[2]	Allen & Overy; Clifford Chance; Freshfields Bruckhaus Deringer;	• Big ticket commercial work – big clients, large deals: mergers and acquisitions (M&A),

[1] It is important to note that every law firm is unique and it is probably unfair to 'box' them into the categories listed in this chapter. One firm may span several 'boxes' and so the above should be used only as a very general guide.

[2] There is much debate as to whether the 'Circle' now includes other firms such as Herbert Smith and Lovells. For arguments sake, we have kept it to five firms.

	Linklaters; Slaughter & May.	disposals, flotations, buy-ins and buyouts, joint ventures, takeovers etc. • Cover a diverse range of practice areas from Corporate and Banking, to Litigation, Employment, IP etc. • International firms with offices overseas. • Trainee intake c.80 - 100 per year (usually split between a March and September intake).
"Mid-sized"	Herbert Smith; Lovells; Simmons & Simmons; Norton Rose; SJ Berwin; Macfarlanes; Travers Smith; Ashursts; CMS Cameron McKenna; Berwin Leighton Paisner; Pinsent Masons; Ince & Co; Taylor Wessing;	• Generally smaller in size than the Magic Circle. • Cover a broad range of practice areas with big clients and big deals. • Trainee intake varies between c.20 - 80 per year and sometimes split over two intakes (September and March). • International firms with offices overseas.

	Watson Farley & Williams.	
"US Firms"	White & Case; Shearman & Sterling; Bingham McCutchen; Clearly Gottlieb Steen & Hamilton; Weil Gotshal & Manges; Skadden Arps.	• Well established in the US but with an ever-increasing presence in the UK. • International firms with overseas offices. • Firm size varies as does trainee intake c. 0 - 30 trainees per year.
"Niche"	Bird and Bird; Bristows; Olswang.	• Cover a range of practice areas but with a strong reputation in a particular specialisation (e.g. Intellectual Property; Media). • Trainee intake c. 5 - 20 per year.
"Regional"	Burges Salmon; Wragge & Co; Walker Morris; Hill Dickinson; Bevan Britten.	• Headquarters located outside of London (but often still have a London office). • Usually only have offices in the UK.

		• Cover a broad range of practice areas but deals (and departments) are generally smaller than those of the larger City firms. • Reputedly better working hours than in the City. • Trainee intake c. 5 – 30 per year.
"High Street"	Joe Bloggs Conveyancing; John Smith and Associates.	• You see them every day on your high street – smaller practices, often only one or two partners. • Generally practice one or two areas of law (Conveyancing, Employment, Family, Immigration, Criminal etc.) and act for smaller clients. • Trainee intake c. 0 – 2 per year.

"In house"	Many large companies will have their own in-house legal team (known as in-house counsel) RBS; Goldman Sachs; Sony; Virgin; Nokia; (...to name but a few!)	• Working in the legal department of a large company, experiencing a wide variety of work. • Very few in-house training contracts available.

SECTION 2:

APPLICATIONS

Qualities Law Firms look for in Prospective Trainees

The list below illustrates, in no particular order, some of the qualities law firms often look for in applicants. It may be useful to use such a list to focus your applications by conveying some of these qualities in your application forms and interviews.

♦ **Intellect**	Many firms look for a consistently high academic record at A-Level and during your degree. Firms usually specify minimum academic requirements (for example, the Magic Circle law firms will typically require a minimum 2:1 degree classification) so check specific firm requirements before applying.
♦ **Ambition/Commitment Determination/Drive** ♦ **Resilience**	A legal career can be difficult and demanding. Your firm may expect a lot from you and you need to demonstrate that you will be able to rise to the challenge.

♦ **Enthusiasm**	You need to convey that you are passionate about your career choice and are excited about the challenges that await you.
♦ **A team player**	As a Solicitor, much of your work will be carried out in teams. You will be required to work alongside a great variety of colleagues and clients.
♦ **Good communication**	You will have to be able to communicate clearly in both written and spoken forms with a variety of colleagues and clients.
♦ **Organisation** ♦ **Flexibility** ♦ **Discipline**	Multi-tasking is a day-to-day aspect of your job as a Solicitor. You must be able to prioritise effectively, often being required to adapt and respond to new ideas and developments.
♦ **Commercial awareness**	This is an extremely important quality to convey in the current legal climate. See our chapter on this at page 63.

♦ **Common sense**	Invaluable in problem solving and when providing useful, practical advice to the client.
♦ **Humour**	Your interviewer will think 'would I enjoy working with this person day to day?' Will they fit into the culture of the firm?
♦ **Outside interests**	Law firms are looking for well-rounded and interesting people.
♦ **Individuality**	Firms want to recruit a variety of individuals. For this reason you should not conform to a pre-conceived stereotype. Always be yourself!
♦ **Professionalism**	Your interviewer will be asking themselves, 'would I be happy to introduce this person to my client/other colleagues'?
♦ **Leadership**	Many firms look for leadership potential. You may find yourself running your own projects very early on in your career.

♦ **Creativity**	You may be required to think of different ways of problem solving and handling difficult situations.
♦ **Integrity**	Trust is an integral part of the relationship between Solicitor and client.

The Application Process

It is never too early to think about applying for vacation schemes and training contracts. The application process can seem both daunting and confusing. It is for this reason that we have put together a quick summary of the key points you need to know.

Overview

- Becoming a Solicitor is very competitive. There are many more people seeking training contracts than there are training contracts available.

- Firms receive hundreds of applications every year for the limited number of places available. Larger firms such as those within the 'Magic Circle' can receive over 1,000 applications and so it is paramount that your application stands out.

How to Apply

- Most of the large firms require applicants to complete an online application form (see page 45 for more details) while some ask for the more traditional CV and covering letter. You will need to find out the specific application requirements from each law firm before you apply (see our Law Firm Directory on page 173).

- If your application / CV and covering letter is successful, you will then be invited to an interview or assessment day with the firm (see pages 69 and 135 for more details). Afterwards, a decision will be made on whether to offer you a place on a vacation scheme/a training contract (depending on which one you are applying for).

When?

- Our timetable on page 169 gives a general overview of the timescale for the recruitment process.

- Training contracts are usually secured 2 years prior to your actual start date. So at the current time of writing (summer 2007), law firms will be recruiting for their 2009/2010 intakes.

- Law students most commonly apply for training contracts in the summer of their penultimate year and non-law students apply in the summer of the last year of their degree course.

- This is obviously only a general rule and is subject to many exceptions. Firms often have last minute vacancies and if you are in a position to start at an earlier date (i.e. you have completed the requisite GDL/LPC) this is often possible. Similarly, if you wish to secure a training contract but then defer your start date for 6 months - 1 year this is often achievable.

A common mistake

- Do not submit your application forms exactly on the deadline which a law firm sets. Both vacation schemes and training contract interviews are often allocated on a "first come first served" basis (as firms do not want to miss out on the best candidates or lose them to their rivals). Moreover, your application form has more chance of standing out when it is not sitting in a pile with 1,000 others that have all been submitted on the last day, so our advice is to apply as early as possible to give yourself the best chance of success.

When will I hear if my application has been successful?

- This will vary greatly between firms.

- Some firms will send you electronic notifications if you are unsuccessful and most will send a letter if you have been invited to an interview/assessment day.

- With regard to training contract places, the Law Society has imposed rules for informing candidates as to whether or not they have been successful. Therefore, following an interview/assessment day, successful candidates who are applying two years prior to their start date, must be informed no earlier than on or after 1 September.

Work Experience

Law firms expect to see some relevant work experience on your application forms/CV if possible. It shows that you know what it is like to work as a Solicitor and are applying for a training contract fully informed and with your eyes open.

A variety of work experience can be beneficial:

- Large firm
- Mid-sized firm
- Regional firm
- High street firm
- Experience in a set of Barristers' chambers

When applying use your different experiences to your advantage. For example, compare different sized firms: "Whilst I enjoyed the intimate and close-knit team atmosphere in [X firm], a small high street practice, it reinforced my belief that I prefer and would be more suited to working in a larger practice. I would enjoy working in larger teams, with a greater variety of clients and practice areas and a more challenging, faster-paced work load. This would, in turn, lead to a more thorough, well-rounded training contract".

I can't secure a vacation scheme...

Don't panic! Believe it or not, it is harder to secure a vacation placement than a training contract (because there are fewer vacation scheme places available and because many people do several vacation schemes in one summer). Law firms are aware of this and will be interested in any legal or commercial work experience you may have gained.

Any commercial experience is good...

Law firms are looking for people with commercial awareness (see page 63) and so any commercial experience, even if totally unrelated to law, will be beneficial. It may be worth considering work experience in a bank, a firm of accountants or any other business that interests you.

Selling your experiences... Tips!

- List your experience in chronological order - starting with the most recent first.

- Use the work experience section of the application form/CV wisely. It is a chance to persuade the firm that you have the skills they are looking for.

- Make the experience personal. Explain what you did during that work placement and the actual tasks you completed. Describe what you learnt and the skills you acquired. (See our list of skills on page 23).

- Use a variety of work experience to persuade the employer that you are making a well-informed decision in choosing to become a Solicitor and in applying to that particular firm.

- Voluntary work experience counts - put it down!

Example...

Organisation: Beckham Rooney Solicitors

Dates: 10/07/07 - 21/07/07

Outline Details/Responsibilities:

Two weeks at Beckham Rooney Solicitors, a commercial practice in Manchester, provided me with a valuable insight into the work undertaken by a commercial Solicitor.

I researched and delivered a presentation to the team on Directors' Duties, attended client meetings, prepared attendance notes and shadowed a partner at an AGM. I was impressed by the complex and challenging nature of the legal work and enjoyed the variety of tasks. I realised the value of team work as much of a Solicitor's work is carried out as part of a larger team working towards a common goal.

During my time with the firm, I also saw the importance of fostering strong client-Solicitor relationships. It was clear how highly clients valued the business-driven legal solutions that a good Solicitor offers.

CVs and Covering Letters

Some firms require your application for a training contract to take the form of a CV (résumé) and covering letter. The key is to keep these succinct and clear. Again, attention to detail is paramount. We have included an example CV and covering letter below together with some tips on how to write them.

CVs

Tips!

- Attention to detail. Check, check and re-check again for typos and spelling errors. Ask a friend to proof read it for you.

- Keep the layout clear, professional and easy to read. Avoid elaborate font styles and formatting.

- Try and keep to a maximum of two A4-sides in length. Use a clear font (e.g. Times, Arial, size 10 - 12).

- Use the same tense throughout. It is advisable to keep to the past tense (e.g. "having worked on...") unless what you are describing is ongoing (e.g. I play squash regularly).

- Avoid jokes and informal use of language. Keep language positive but professional.

- Be succinct. Avoid unnecessary words.

- Dates (for education and work experience history) should be in chronological order - most recent first.

- Do not leave gaps in dates. A missing year in your education history will raise eyebrows!

- Do not lie! Ever.

- Be honest about your exam results - it is likely that they will check your marks with your academic referee.

- Use the descriptive sections (work experience, interests and achievements) to sell yourself to the employer. Illustrate skills that you have acquired and make your experiences and descriptions personal to you.

Example:

CURRICULUM VITAE

ROBERT MARLEY

17 Paradise Beach Avenue
London E3 9TF
Home Tel. 01234 567 890
Mobile. 07788 999 999
bobmarley@hotmeal.com
DOB: 06/02/1945
Nationality: Jamaican

EDUCATION

2006-2007 **Graduate Diploma in Law - Nottingham Law School**

2003-2006 **B.A. in Music, Queens College, Leeds (2:1 achieved)**
Average marks: First Year (58%), Second Year (61%), Third Year (65%)

2001-2003 **St Johns School, Kent**
A-Levels: Music (A), French (B), Maths (C)

1999-2001 **St Johns School, Kent**
GCSEs: (5As), (3Bs), (1C)

WORK EXPERIENCE

Summer 2006 (2 weeks) — **Vacation Scheme – Paul Moss Solicitors, London**

- Carried out research on Powers of Arrest under time pressured conditions and gave a presentation to the team on my findings.
- Attended client meetings and took clear and concise attendance notes.
- Saw in practice the variety of work undertaken by Solicitors on a daily basis.
- Enjoyed the complex and challenging nature of legal work and the satisfaction in providing practical solutions to clients.

Easter 2005 (1 week) — **Work experience at Acorns Accountancy, Kent**

- Attended meetings and welcomed clients at reception. Obtained an insight into the commercial workings of a non-law firm. Reinforced my belief that I am more interested in, and more suited to, a career in law.

Ongoing — **Volunteer for Oxfam**

- Working in my local Oxfam shop enables me to interact with a diverse cross section of society and allows me to give something back to my local community.
- Participating in fundraising events (such as a fun-run around my local park) provides a refreshing change to my studies whilst helping to raise money for charity.

Various	**Law firm open days:** Clifford Chance, London Burges Salmon, Bristol

LANGUAGES

French	Intermediate
German	Basic

INTERESTS AND ACHIEVEMENTS

Positions of responsibility - As a Senior Prefect, I organised school events such as assemblies and sports days. I liaised with teachers and the governing body to persuade them to improve various aspects of school life such as increased access to school computers and an improved careers service. Having been elected to the Ball Committee by my peers, I helped organise a Charity Ball, in particular organising posters and flyers and the sale of tickets. We managed to attract 100 guests and raised £5,500 for charity.

Music - I enjoy playing the guitar and am a member of a band which performs for various events such as weddings and birthday parties.

Sport - As captain of the B-squad football team, I am able to increase my fitness levels as well as improve my teamwork and leadership skills.

REFEREES

Academic
Professor Elvis
Personal Tutor
Queens College, Leeds
Kings Street
L1 1NJ
elvisp@queens.ac.uk

Other:
Barry White
Oxfam
3 Soho Square
London
W1 LOV
b.white@oxfam.com

Covering letters

Tips!

- As a general rule, whenever sending your CV to an employer, it should be accompanied by a covering letter. The aim of the letter is to explain why you are sending the CV, but a good covering letter should highlight your skills and experience and persuade the employer to interview you.

- Think about the information you wish to convey in your covering letter. It should be succinct, to the point and well structured. A useful way of structuring your letter could be as follows:

    - **In paragraph 1**: Introduce yourself, your background and explain that you are applying for a training contract/vacation scheme.

    - **In paragraph 2**: Use this for the main content. Describe the experience you have (work/non-academic achievements/other) and explain how those experiences make you suitable for the role (i.e. what skills or insights you have gained).

    - **In paragraph 3**: Explain why you have chosen that particular firm.

- Keep it formal and professional.

- Length - generally not longer than one page (of size 10-12, Times New Roman or Arial font).

- Print the letter (together with your CV) on good quality paper. Do not photocopy it.

- Attention to detail. Check, check and re-check again for typos and spelling errors. Ask a friend to proof read it for you.

- Address it to the correct person (if you know the name of the recipient) and ensure their name and title are correct.

- See page 145 for our basic guide to letter writing to ensure you start and end your letter correctly.

Example:

Mr. Tom Jones
Linkfields Solicitors
10 New Square
London
E12 9GF

12 May 2007

Dear Mr. Jones,

Having attended an open day at Linkfields Solicitors last year, I was thoroughly impressed by the firm and am now applying for a training contract with you to commence in September 2010. I am currently a second year student studying for the 3-year LLB Law degree at King's College, London.

During my degree, I gained experience working in a small criminal law firm where I had an opportunity to work on individual cases with minimal supervision. I was able to provide assistance to Solicitors in preparing client notes and drafting attendance notes. Last summer I undertook a mini pupillage at the chambers of Andrew Dent QC which I thoroughly enjoyed but which strengthened my commitment to qualifying as a Solicitor. I realised that I would be more suited to working as part of a team on transactional deals that I could be involved in from start to completion. Whilst I enjoyed the supportive team atmosphere and high degree of responsibility that working at a regional firm in Bristol provided, I now feel I am making an informed decision in applying to a larger commercial firm with a more diverse range of practice areas and a greater support network. I would enjoy the chance to work for some of your major clients on complex and challenging deals.

I am applying to Linkfields Solicitors because of your unrivalled reputation in the field of Commercial and Banking law, illustrated by your consistently high ranking in the Legal 500. I would relish the opportunity to learn from and work with some of the best lawyers in their fields of specialisation and am impressed by the quality of training you offer. I believe that my strong academic record and practical legal experience, combined with a genuine enthusiasm for the law, will enable me to make a valuable contribution to your firm. I enclose my CV for your consideration and look forward to hearing from you shortly.

If there is any further information you require, please do not hesitate to contact me.

Yours sincerely,

Robert Marley

Enc.

Application Form Tips

Application forms can be long and daunting. Rejoice in the knowledge that once you have completed one, the rest become easier so it is worth taking your time to begin with. Ensure you make the most of every section of the form. Use it to persuade the employer why you are suitable to both the firm and the position you are applying for. Here are some quick tips for success.

1. Attention to detail – spelling/grammar/punctuation

As a trainee your attention to detail will be constantly tested. Many firms will reject a form if they spot a typo. At the very least, it will create a negative impression and aggravate your reader.

2. Brain storm!

Before filling out your form, think about the skills the employer is looking for (see page 23 onwards for ideas) and how you can demonstrate those skills using personal examples.

3. Answer the question!

Do not write an answer to a question you wish you had been asked or that you have prepared for another form! Splitting the question into its component parts can often help focus the mind and ensure that you have provided a complete answer.

4. Use a range of examples

Use a range of examples from your hobbies, work experience and academic achievements to answer the questions. Make sure that these are fairly recent examples from the last few years (that starring role as a Shepherd in your school Nativity will (sadly) have to be omitted!).

5. Structure your answer

This will set your form apart and shows that you have carefully thought about your answer. Think about the component parts of the question and cover those parts in the same order in your answer. (See examples below.) It may help to think of each answer as if you are telling a story, with a start, middle and end. For example, 'What did you do? How did you do it? What was the outcome and what did you learn?' Although the aforementioned may sound too simplistic, it is surprising how many people fail to provide logical well-structured answers to even the most basic questions.

6. Follow instructions

If the form asks for a particular format, then make sure that you follow it! If it asks for a 200 word answer, stick to it. Send your form to the correct person and by the stipulated deadline.

7. Don't lie!

It is dishonest and you risk being caught out at a later stage (whether in an interview or once you are actually with the firm undertaking a vacation scheme or training contract). It is possible that if you put down on your CV that you speak Spanish to a high level, someone at your interview will launch into a conversation in Spanish with you and you will be left floundering. Remember that it is possible to present all experiences in a positive light.

8. Be clear and concise

Do not attach hundreds of additional sheets. Answer the questions in the spaces provided – word limits are there for a reason. If you need to explain a part of your application in more detail, put it in a covering letter and attach it to your form.

9. Keep it specific and personal

Do not simply list skills. Use specific examples from your experiences to illustrate those skills. Avoid generic answers, they will not engage your reader or offer an insight into why they should choose you in particular. Instead, make your answers as personal as possible by saying 'why', 'how' etc.

10. Make it relevant to the firm

Do not cut and paste from one form to the next – you risk talking about a competitor by accident and not answering the specific questions contained in each form. Make a conscious effort to include that particular firm's distinguishing factors as often as possible and explain why you have chosen that firm as opposed to any other.

11. Print off a completed copy of the form

You will need to study the form and remind yourself of its contents before any interview you may attend.

Remember the application form contains all the information the interviewers will have about you and they will undoubtedly ask you questions based around what you have provided.

Application Forms
Questions and Model Answers

We have chosen some of the most frequently asked questions and provided model answers below[3]. This should give you a good idea of structure and content. As long as you carefully plan what information you will include, write clear, succinct answers and follow our tips on pages 45 - 48, what initially look like a daunting array of questions suddenly become more manageable. Once you have completed one form you will discover that many firms ask very similar (but not identical) questions. It is worth, therefore, taking time over your first few forms.

1. What attracted you to [X firm] in particular?

- **Reputation** - Awards, Chambers & Partners/Legal 500.
- **Clients** - Research major clients/recent deals.
- **High quality work/training and lawyers** - Learning and working with the best lawyers in your peer group/the City.
- **Culture** - Supportive, friendly, open-door, good work-life balance, extra-curricular and pro-bono activities.

[3] These answers are for illustrative purposes only and should not be copied.

- **High retention rate for Newly Qualified Solicitors ("NQs")** - Long term career prospects.

- **International focus** - Opportunities for secondments, communicating and working with lawyers/clients from across the globe.

- **Diverse practice areas/better breadth of training** - more varied and well-rounded training with a larger choice as to an eventual area of specialisation.

- **Support network** - supervisors, mentors, secretaries, word processing assistants, paralegals, professional support lawyers ("PSLs").

2. Why have you chosen a career in commercial law?

(Max. 250 words)

- Show that you are interested in the subject. My first insight into the legal profession was during:

    - the work experience at [x]
    - the vacation scheme at [x]
    - my studies (give brief details)

- Through my experiences, I was attracted to a legal career, particularly in commercial law, because I would enjoy:

    - the intellectual challenge;
    - diverse and constantly evolving subject matter;
    - the interesting and varied work, training and client base;
    - working within a team to achieve a common goal;
    - the good career prospects and clarity in career progression;
    - working alongside like-minded people who are ambitious, driven and enjoy a challenge;
    - the international dimension/potential to use language skills/travel/ability to work with lawyers from across the globe;[4] and
    - the financial rewards and benefits.

3. What makes you suited to a legal career?

[4] Only applicable to international firms.

Demonstrate some or all of the following using a mix of your own personal experiences:

- Academic ability
- Enthusiasm
- Motivation/drive/resilience
- Hard-working
- Organisation and discipline
- Team-player
- Confidence
- Willingness to accept responsibility
- Results-driven
- Committed
- Common sense
- Sense of humour
- Ambition
- Good communication skills (both written and oral)
- Good interpersonal skills
- Professional
- Strong commercial acumen.

4. How would you ensure that [X firm] maintains a high standard of client care?

- Competitive pricing (discounts for loyalty/volume of work).

- Effective communication (keeping the client informed at all stages).

- High quality service (fast, accurate, efficient, flexible and tailored to the client's business needs).

- Practical, business driven solutions given in light of a good understanding of the client's business and an appreciation of the market in which that business operates.

- Designated relationship partner/primary contact point for client to call at any time.

- Second lawyers to clients (either trainees or Solicitors).

- Free legal updates/in-house training.

- Client entertainment - focus on fostering long-term client relationships.

- Client feedback policy - questionnaire/phone call every 6 months to enquire about the service the client has received and highlight any areas that need to be improved upon.

5. What has been your greatest challenge, how did you overcome it and what did you learn?

(Max. 250 words)

- Background/set the scene

- Describe the challenge and why it was difficult

- How did you overcome it? (skills employed)
- Outcome (the success)
- What you learnt

Example 1:

- During my gap year, I applied to take part in a volunteering expedition to Malawi to assist with a building project within a local community.

- The challenge was to raise £3,000 in order to fund the expedition.

- I overcame this by undertaking various fundraising activities, the largest of which was organising a musical concert at my school. This required me to be organised, motivated and determined. My determination and resilience were also tested particularly because it took much longer and was much harder to reach my target than I had initially anticipated.

- Fortunately I managed to raise the £3,000 in the required timescale and participated in the house building project.

- Although the expedition was hard work and challenging (requiring us to build in relentless heat most days), I felt I was part of a fantastic, eye-opening experience. I learnt a lot about a new country and culture, made some life-long friends and, most importantly, it was rewarding to give something back to a local community.

Example 2:

- It had always been an ambition of mine to play sport as part of a team, albeit an area in which I had never excelled at school.

- At the start of my lower sixth year at school I made the decision to train hard with the aim of being selected to play for one of my school's rugby teams.

- I joined the local gym which I attended four times a week and signed up for all the after-school and lunchtime rugby training sessions.

- After two terms, my fitness, strength, and tactical ability had improved significantly and I was delighted to be selected to play for the School 3rd Team at Full Back.

- I learnt that through perseverance, motivation and hard-work, any goal is achievable. Playing sport as part of a team is extremely rewarding and during the last month of my lower sixth year I was thrilled to be asked to captain the 3rd team during my upper sixth year.

6. Please provide us with any additional information in support of your application.

This question appears at the end of most application forms and is your opportunity to add any additional/supporting evidence and provide a rounded conclusion to your application.

But remember:-

- Do not repeat yourself.
- Do not write an essay - this section should be short and succinct.
- This will be the last section that is read so ensure you leave a good and lasting impression.

<u>Example:</u>

I am wholly committed to a career in law. I believe that my strong academic record, practical legal experience and overriding enthusiasm for the law will provide me with the solid foundations necessary to embark on a career as a commercial City Solicitor. I would relish the opportunity to train at a firm of such high calibre and international standing as [X firm] where such an excellent training would provide for a long term and dedicated career with the firm.

7. Please explain why you have chosen to work in [Bristol].

- Try to avoid using the word 'provincial' or 'regional'- this can anger non-London based firms who may consider the terms patronising.

- Emphasise the strength of your links to the particular city/area (e.g. school/ university/ friends/family).

- Provide convincing evidence of your long-term commitment to the firm/city/area.

- Explain why you are not interested in working in London (e.g. you prefer working in smaller teams, more diverse range of work, higher amount of client contact at an early stage in your career etc.).

8. Describe an event that has recently been in the news, why has this been of interest to you?

I have been following the recent merger discussions surrounding the major music companies in the UK.

Most recently, EMI has been the subject of a takeover bid by the equity house Terra Firma, together with speculation of a competing offer from Warner Music Group. This has been interesting due to the competition issues arising from a potential merger between EMI and Warner (in light of the recent anti-trust investigations into the Sony-BMG merger).

This deal encapsulates the recent economic difficulties that the large music companies face in a world of increasing digitalisation and piracy and their need to find new ways of becoming more competitive in such an aggressive music market.

9. Please give an overview of your main interests, hobbies, awards and achievements including any voluntary work and outlining positions of responsibility.

(Max. 250 words)

- This question is asking for a lot of information and is testing your ability to structure a clear and succinct answer.
- Make the question applicable/personal to yourself and your experiences - you do not have to have won a Nobel Prize or lifted the F.A. Cup.
- Use this question to convey particular skills, both personal and professional.

Example:

A passion for art provides an outlet for my creativity, while playing on my university hockey team enables me to keep fit as well as learn important teamwork skills. This year I was particularly proud of being nominated for 'Player of the Season' by my peers.

I recently completed my bronze Duke of Edinburgh Award which was a huge but satisfying challenge. As part of this I volunteered in my local old people's home, which improved my listening and communication skills.

I was a prefect at school for four years liaising closely with teachers and pupils alike and organising a number of school events such as school discos and sports days. This was challenging but extremely rewarding as I was able to interact with students of all ages and have a voice in key aspects of school life.

I have always enjoyed travelling, most recently backpacking around Europe with friends. This enabled me to broaden my horizons and learn about different cultures and traditions.

10. Describe a situation which has demonstrated your ability to deal with setbacks and cope effectively with conflict and pressure.

(Max. 200 words)

[Background]

During my A-Levels I took part in The Young Enterprise Scheme being elected to the position of Marketing Director within our events company. Our main project was to organise a charity fashion show.

[Setback]

Three weeks before the show four key members of the company resigned. They felt their ideas were not being considered and the company was taking a direction that they were unhappy with. The company and the entire project were at risk of collapse with months of hard work likely to be wasted.

[Solution]

I resolved to deal with the problem diplomatically by organising a meeting complete with a short agenda addressing the key issues. This helped to focus the discussion and ensure we resolved each issue systematically. During the meeting I took on the role of Chairman and ensured that everyone had the chance to air their opinions equally. I re-emphasised to the group that the overriding aim of the project was to raise money for charity, a worthy goal. After a lengthy discussion and a vote on the major issues with concessions made by both sides, the company successfully ran the fashion show. We were delighted to make a total of £2,000 for Barnardos.

(196 words)

Additional example questions:

11. At [X Firm] you will be expected to work with a wide range of people and to be able to persuade, influence and display effective communication skills. Please demonstrate your experience of these skills.

12. Please outline a problem that you have solved by offering an alternative solution; what steps did you take? How did you implement it? (200 words)

13. Please provide details of any positions of responsibility you have held. What did you learn about yourself and your impact on others?

14. Which areas of your degree interested you most and which did you find most difficult? Give your reasons. (200 words)

15. How does a legal career compare with other possible career choices you have considered? (200 words)

16. Please describe a situation where you had to deal with competing demands on your time and which required you to be well-organised as well as detail conscious. (200 words)

17. What do you believe has been the key to [X firm's] success? How might the firm continue this success? (400 words)

18. What challenges might commercial law firms and commercial businesses face over the next 5 years? (400 words)

Commercial Awareness Tips

What is 'commercial awareness'?
Although recruiters use this term a lot, it is difficult to know exactly what it means. If you have been desperately searching for an answer, look no further! We have scaled the highest mountains and tackled the most fearsome beasts (HR managers) to bring the following pearls of wisdom to your doorstep...

What is it?

Commercial awareness is a skill most legal employers will expect you to have as a trainee Solicitor. They will want you to demonstrate your commercial knowledge throughout the application process.

In broad terms, it is your ability to see things from a commercial or business perspective. A law firm's business is driven by the needs of its clients. An essential skill of any lawyer, therefore, is the ability to understand its client's business as a whole, not just the legal problem it is faced with. Clients do not want a technical legal essay in answer to their problem, they require a business solution that is practical and that appreciates the commercial context in which that business operates.

To help understand the commercial context to a problem, it is useful to consider who the main stakeholders are and think about what their concerns might be. Stakeholders may include: customers, employees, directors, shareholders, investors and legal and financial advisors.

How do you show you have it?

Do not fear, owning your own FTSE 100 Company is not essential!

Other ways it can be shown is through the following:

- **Work experience**

  Perhaps you have worked in a shop or some other commercial enterprise that has taught you about customers - what they expect and how to please them. Through work experience you may have gained some understanding about the difficulties businesses face such as competition, supply and demand issues, cash flow problems, customers and employee satisfaction etc.

- **Extra-curricular interests**

  You may have helped organise a school event, been part of a committee in charge of marketing, sales or finance, or been a member of a Young Enterprise Scheme at school. Any of these, or similar, experiences may have provided you with an insight into how a successful business is run.

- **Travel**

  Even your travel experiences can contribute to good commercial awareness. Many businesses, especially law firms, are becoming more and more international in scope. Travel can give you a different perspective on the world. It broadens your mind, giving invaluable insights into different cultures and traditions that co-exist alongside each other in every day life.

- **Application forms/interviews/case studies**

  Law firm application forms may ask you to describe a deal in the press that has interested you. This is designed to test your commercial awareness (see our example on page 57). Similarly, at interview, you may be presented with a case study. You will be asked questions based on the study to illustrate your awareness of the key commercial issues. (See pages 138 - 141 for an example case study.)

How do I improve my commercial awareness?

The best way to improve your commercial awareness is to read newspapers and legal publications (The Financial Times, The Economist, The Times, The Guardian, The Lawyer and Legal Week, to name but a few). Research current hot topics and generally gain an awareness of what is going on in the business world.

Before your interview, find out about recent significant deals in the press so that you can talk intelligently about them at interview if prompted. It is always useful to research one particular deal that you have found interesting and to think about who the deal affects and why it is so significant.

Undertake work experience in any commercial enterprise – it could be a law firm, bank, restaurant or anywhere that has customers or is run like a business.

SECTION 3:

INTERVIEWS AND ASSESSMENT CENTRES

Interview Tips

Congratulations! You've secured that interview and now it's time to impress in person. The key to success is in the preparation. The more prepared you are, the more confident you will feel and this will come across in the interview. Remember that your interviewer is not the enemy. You have already impressed them on paper and they are not trying to catch you out. They WANT you to be good to save them having to interview more candidates.

1. DO YOUR HOMEWORK!

Review your application/CV before the interview - be prepared to talk about and back up everything you have written. Research as much as you can about the firm (such as its main clients, size and where it has offices) so that you can talk about why you are suitable to the firm and what it is about the firm that you are attracted to.

Try and gauge from your research how the firm sees itself in the market. For example, if it sees itself as on a par with the Magic Circle sized firms, do not talk about the firm as a 'mid-sized' firm in your interview. It is important that your perception of the firm matches what the interviewers think and want to hear.

2. Appearance

Dress correctly, remember that first impressions last!

The following is advisable... wear a neutral, dark suit with polished shoes. Women should ensure hair and nails are tidy and always wear tights with skirt suits (even in the summer). Keep your jacket done up (and don't take it off unless you are told you can do so). If you are travelling from elsewhere in the country and have bags with you, make sure you leave any excess luggage you have at reception instead of hauling it into the interview with you.

3. Allow plenty of time for your journey

Public transport is always out to get you when you are in a rush. It's obvious - be late, and you will already have made a bad impression.

Having enough time to take a last minute look at your notes on the firm combined with a shot of espresso while you wait nervously in the coffee shop outside could be the difference between success and failure!

4. When meeting the interviewers: give a strong handshake, maintain eye contact and SMILE!

A bit like patting your head and rubbing your tummy - seems simple until you try it. Avoid the wet lettuce hand shake and shifty looking stare. If possible, find out who is interviewing you beforehand and try and read up about them and the recent deals they have been involved in on the firm's website.

5. Speak clearly, be confident but not arrogant

Firms are looking for someone who can speak easily and appear professional. They will understand that you will be a bit nervous. Try having a practise interview with someone you do not know well to hone your skills in this area (your careers department should help you with this).

6. Don't fidget

Try and relax. Sit comfortably without slouching and avoid crossing your arms (as this can appear hostile). Minimise nervous twitching, fiddling and hair flicking!

7. Pre-empt questions and prepare answers before the interview

See our questions on page 75 onwards. Think of the kind of questions the firm is likely to ask and prepare good outline answers (do not learn word-for-word answers as they will sound too rehearsed). When those questions come up at interview, you will be able to deliver confident, well structured answers. The interviewer will be impressed because it will appear as if you have thought up an excellent answer on the spot!

8. Answer the question and try not to waffle

Take your time and answer the precise question asked. Going off on a tangent will not impress. If you don't know the answer, don't talk about something completely different. If you did not understand the question, it is okay to ask for clarification. Once you have given a complete answer, stop! Don't be tempted to keep talking indefinitely about an unrelated matter.

9. What if I don't know the answer?

Be honest but positive. Say that you don't know the answer but would like to make an educated guess. Or, if relevant, explain how you would go about finding the answer or that you would be interested to find out. This will impress your interviewers far more than if you try to bluff your way through an answer when it is clear you do not understand.

10. There is often no right or wrong answer

Instead, the interviewer is looking to see how you argue, structure and defend a point raised. They will also test your ability to think on your feet. Do not be flustered if the interviewers seem aggressive, they are merely testing your ability to cope under pressure and when challenged. Remain calm and offer a cool, reasoned response in line with your original stance.

11. Use a variety and balance of examples to back up your answers

Think of good examples from your hobbies, work experience and academic achievements that you could use in interviews. It is important to use the best example you can for each question, but ensure this is not the same one for every answer. Again, pre-interview preparation here is key.

12. Always ask the interviewer questions

Astute, thoughtful questions are a way of showing the interviewer you have done your homework and are switched-on (see our list of example questions from page 121 onwards). Do not ask questions you could have easily found out yourself (e.g. by reading the firm's website) unless you can put an original and thoughtful slant on them.

Remember this is also your chance to find out information about the firm that you are genuinely interested in and which might help you make a decision as to which firm you will eventually work for.

Finally…

Learn from your experiences

Practice makes perfect. You may or may not have been successful at one particular interview but either way the experience will have taught you a lot (even if it may not seem that way at first!).

Reflect on what went well and what you need to improve on so that the next interview is even more polished. Many employers will offer interview feedback to unsuccessful candidates so it is always worth giving them a call.

Good luck!

200 Interview Questions

The questions you could be faced with during an interview will vary greatly from one law firm to another. One interview could be highly structured with a case study and lots of questions testing your commercial awareness and commitment to law. Other interviews may feel more like an informal 'chat' focusing on your interests and hobbies.

Below are some of the questions you may be asked during an interview together with some model answers[5].

1. Why law?

2. Why a Solicitor and not a Barrister?

Here are a few suggestions:

- You prefer working in larger teams on ongoing deals. Barristers tend to work alone more often.
- Large firms offer a well structured training programme with the chance to sample a broad variety of practice areas (or 'seats') – enabling you to make a more informed decision when choosing an area of specialisation on completion of your training contract.

[5] These questions and model answers are illustrative only and their content may be deemed controversial in some contexts. Please use them only as a guide and not as a substitute for your own careful research.

- Law firms have great support systems in place (from good paralegal and secretarial support to in-house restaurants, doctors and dentists) allowing you to do your job more effectively.

- You would prefer to join a big intake of trainees rather than just one or two fellow new recruits. Again, this provides greater support and creates an immediate social and business network.

- You prefer the work Solicitors undertake – perhaps more transactional in nature with the opportunity to work on deals from start to finish. (Barristers may only see snippets of the deal as they are drafted in for stand-alone pieces of advice.)

- You would like the opportunity to go on an international or client secondment.

- If you enjoy standing up and arguing in court, as a Solicitor there is still the opportunity to do this by obtaining your 'Higher Rights of Audience' and many firms will sponsor you to obtain this qualification.

- Many Barristers work on a self-employed basis, relying on you to develop a good client base rather than receiving an annual salary. You would rather work for a large employer with a regular, more certain income (especially as a junior lawyer) and a better benefits package.

3. Why this firm?

4. I see you did work experience at [Z firm] a high street criminal law firm [*or other firm*] and enjoyed it. Why, then, do you wish to work for [X firm] a large commercial practice?

Take care not to be disparaging about other firms (it only makes you look unprofessional and indiscreet). Talk about all your experiences in a positive light (e.g. "Whilst I enjoyed my experience at [Z firm], I nevertheless…") and describe what you gained from it, and what more you think you will gain from working at [X firm]. Explain why you are attracted to, as well as suited to, that specific commercial firm (what factors set it apart from its competitors). Perhaps you are attracted to their unique training system or the number of seats they offer. Perhaps you like the particular type of work they do, or the pro bono (free) work they support. There are countless ways of distinguishing one firm from the next and this is where researching the firm thoroughly before your interview is essential.

E.g. Whilst I thoroughly enjoyed my work experience at [Z firm] (a 'high street' firm), I believe I would enjoy and be more suited to working at a larger commercial practice like [X Firm]. At the high street practice, I appreciated the strong team culture and high degree of responsibility that I was given, however I believe that these are qualities I could equally find at [X firm]. I think I would be more suited to a larger practice because of the greater variety of work and practice areas that you offer which would provide me with a more diverse and well-rounded training contract. I am attracted to your 4 seat system of training which (unlike the 6 or 7 seat systems offered by some firms) would enable me to become thoroughly absorbed into each department's work as well as fully integrated into the team before I was required to move onto the next seat. I would appreciate the greater support system that a firm like yours has to offer, such as the 24-hour secretarial and paralegal support (meaning less time photocopying and more time focusing on more challenging and interesting fee-earning work). I would also enjoy being part of a larger team, working alongside and learning from some of the best lawyers in their fields of specialisation and working on high value, challenging projects for big-name clients such as [*X, Y, Z - research who their biggest clients are*].

5. What have you found most interesting in your studies? Why?

6. What did you find most difficult in your studies? Why?

7. Why have you applied to us (given the other very different firms you have applied to)? What distinguishes our firm from all of the others?

8. Why do you want to work in the City? Why not a smaller, less busy town or city? Why not a high street employment law 9-5pm practice?

9. Who else have you applied to and why?

10. Describe something that has caught your eye in the press recently [*ideally a commercial transaction*]. Tell us about it. Why does it interest you?

I have been following the recent merger discussions surrounding the major music companies in the UK.

Most recently, EMI has been the subject of a takeover bid by the equity house Terra Firma, together with speculation of a competing offer from Warner Music Group. This has been interesting due to the competition issues arising from a potential merger between EMI and Warner (in light of the recent anti-trust investigations into the Sony-BMG merger).

This deal encapsulates the recent economic difficulties that the large music companies face in a world of increasing digitalisation and piracy and their need to find new ways of becoming more competitive in such an aggressive music market.

11. What do you hope to gain from training at this firm?

12. Why do you think you would be suited to this firm?

13. What skills/qualities could you contribute to this firm?

14. What do think about the recent interest rate increase? Who does this effect?

15. Why was your Contract law exam mark much lower than the other marks? Did you not enjoy the subject?

16. You've just won the lottery, how would you invest £10million?

This question is looking to test both your business acumen and general knowledge of the financial markets.

- The key is to have a diverse portfolio of investment in order to spread the risk.
- The stock market continues to outperform all other kinds of investment in terms of returns, as a long-term strategy. Ensure that shareholdings are spread across a range of industries, again, to protect against downturns in any specific sector.
- Property remains a sound investment, particularly in the long-term. The buy-to-let market is still strong and produces excellent returns.
- Make use of tax-free savings (maximum amount in ISA's per year).
- Put a large amount of savings into a Pension to ensure the maximum amount of tax relief.
- Establish a fund for my children's education. (Private education costs have been rising faster than inflation and University education is likely to be more expensive in future).

17. What makes a good lawyer? How can you prove that you have those qualities?

18. What makes a bad lawyer?

19. What do you think about the growing number of US firms in the UK? They pay a lot - why don't you want to work for one?

- Much can be said about the increasing presence of US law firms in the UK, but here are some ideas to get you started.

- Ten years ago, the presence of US law firms in the UK was not as significant as it is now and many City firms did not consider them to be a big threat. US firms had much smaller offices, often with only a few lawyers specialising in a finite number of subject areas and with a less well-established reputation in the UK.

- Today there are a number of well established US firms in the UK. Some US firms are large and compete heavily with the biggest City law firms for both work and the best graduates. Firms such as White & Case recruit a large number of trainees every year, other US firms still recruit no trainees or perhaps only a couple of trainees each year.

- It is true that many of the US firms pay more than other City firms, but some people believe that you are required to work longer hours for it.

- You should not focus on the size of your pay cheque when answering this question. Emphasize that your choice of which firm to join is based primarily on more important factors such as the training it has to offer, the working atmosphere, culture and reputation of the firm, the variety of work available, the support system in place and the likelihood of being offered a job upon completing your training contract (to name but a few).

20. How do you keep up with current affairs?

21. Trainees are often expected to work long hours on fairly uninteresting pieces of work - even partners can end up photocopying and proof reading. You say you like the thrill of high profile, high value deals. How does this fit in with your idea of being a trainee? Are you not going to be bored?

This question is testing your understanding of the role of a trainee within a firm and your enthusiasm for the tasks that trainees are often faced with, therefore a competent answer might go along the following lines:

I understand that the role of a trainee encompasses a wide variety of work and that sometimes this will include an element of photocopying/proof reading and other less challenging tasks. However, I believe that as long as I am busy I will not be bored. Moreover, I am aware of the importance of seeing the bigger picture and the fact that even the more menial tasks are important within the context of a deal as a whole.

I am also a great believer in the fact that you can get yourself as involved as you want and you can choose to learn as much as you want from any given task. Therefore, I would push myself to learn as much as possible at every stage, even from the most basic proof-reading. I also regard myself as enthusiastic and motivated and these qualities would ensure that I was fully engaged with the task at hand.

22. What kind of work do you think a trainee does?

23. What sort of work would a trainee be expected to undertake on a large Corporate deal?

24. Where do you see yourself in 5 years?

25. Where do you see yourself in 10 years?

In asking this question, the interviewer wants to see you have thought of a long-term career strategy and that you are not applying to be a Solicitor on a whim:

- Working as a Solicitor at the pinnacle of my career, hopefully as a partner. Working with like-minded peers and for a diverse range of clients.

- Having my own clients, a strong and trusted relationship with them, and being a well respected member of the legal profession.

- Finding my work both interesting and enjoyable.

- Having returned to the UK following some time spent working abroad, ideally in Asia as I've always held an ambition to work in Hong Kong or Tokyo.

- Ideally with a Golf Handicap of scratch having spent many more hours on the Golf course!

26. You say you know our firm well - who are our biggest clients?

27. The work we do is done in teams. Are you a leader or a follower? Which do you think is more important?

28. Have you got any experience of working in a team?

29. What makes a good team player?

- Willingness to get involved;

- Ability to take and follow instructions;

- Good sense of humour;

- Understanding the needs and jobs of others.

30. We take special care when selecting supervisors for our trainees. Sometimes people have bad days. How would you deal with a difficult supervisor?

31. Sometimes we are asked to do jobs we do not want to do/we think should be given to someone else. How would you react to this?

32. A client calls you and says they need an answer to a question immediately otherwise they will go to [a competitor]. Your supervisor is away. You think you know the answer from your law school studies. What do you do?

This question is looking to test your common sense. DO NOT pretend that you are a partner and say to the client that you know the answer and start reeling off everything you think you can remember from law school. You are not qualified to give this advice. Remain calm and politely request the client's name and contact number and explain that your colleague will be in touch very shortly to assist him. Then quickly find a partner or senior associate in your team, explain the situation and its urgency and they should take it from there. Offer your help to that partner or associate – they may require you to do some urgent research.

33. What makes a bad team player?

34. A client calls you and demands to speak to your supervisor. Your supervisor is out of the office and tells you he cannot take calls all day. What do you do?

35. A document arrives in your inbox. It is clearly sent in error and not intended for your eyes. It contains all the arguments the other side intend to use and will help your side win the case. What do you do?

36. You've just managed to drink away your weekly allowance at the pub and can't afford to eat for the rest of the month but amazingly find £200 on the bus in a tatty looking envelope? What do you do?

I understand how important the qualities of honesty and integrity are within society and particularly within the legal profession so I would obviously take the £200 to the nearest police station and report it lost or stolen.

37. It is the day before your first Finals exam. You've not had any sleep from worry and you have left your revision too late but only because you have been counselling a family member. You probably will not pass. A friend has managed to get hold of a copy of the exam paper and offers you a look (you think it is probably not real anyway). What do you do?

38. You say an important quality in a Solicitor is organisational skill. How do you stay organised?

39. Tell us about your work experience at [X firm]. What did you like about it? What did you dislike/what would you improve?

40. I see you like to travel. Why so? What have you learnt from the countries you have visited?

41. If you are unable to secure a training contract this year, what will you do?

This question wants to make sure that you have got adequate contingency plans, but are committed to a career in law.

If I were unsuccessful in securing a training contract this year, I would look into what I could do to enhance my skill set and therefore my chances of success next year. This might include the following:

- Paralegal work: I believe this would be a great way of getting to understand what it would be like to work within the legal environment and gain some great experience at the same time.

- Enrolling on an evening language course. I speak basic French but would relish the opportunity to improve to a more competent level. I am aware that in light of the increasingly global nature of the economy, language skills are an excellent asset to possess and will assist me throughout my career.

- Working within industry - as lawyers have to offer increasingly business-driven solutions, I think it would be of much value to spend some time working within an industry, particularly banking and finance, which I have a specific interest in and which is so closely linked to the legal market.

42. Why did you choose to study at [X] university?

43. Why didn't you choose to apply to Oxford or Cambridge? (*where applicable*)

44. Why did you choose your A-Levels? (Other than the fact you enjoyed those subjects the most?)

45. How would you prioritise competing tasks all of which seemed urgent?

- Key to effective organisation is to keep the channels of communication open.

- This is particularly applicable when working as a trainee and when you have work from a variety of different people, each of whom do not know of the competing deadline of any other fee-earner.

- Need to go and see each fee-earner and explain the situation and tell them about the different pieces of work and re-order with a clear 'to-do' list keeping all parties updated as much as possible with your progress and changing timescale.

46. A good Solicitor needs to be able to think on their feet using their initiative and to be able to react quickly to changing circumstances. How can you demonstrate this quality?

47. Have you completed any summer vacation schemes? What did you learn about law firms during your time at [X firm]?

48. Tell us about the work you did during your vacation scheme at [X firm]. Did you find the work interesting? Why so?

49. If you end up with more than one training contract offer, how will you choose between the different firms? What criteria will you use?

1. **Quality of Work** - firm's reputation, breadth of practice areas, client base.

2. **Culture/People** – collegiate, supportive atmosphere, open-door policy, friendly, outgoing team-orientated departments.

3. **Career Prospects** – International opportunities, standard of training.

Overall I would choose the firm that I felt fitted in best with my personality and aspirations and the firm at which I felt I could excel to the greatest degree.

50. Would you like to be a partner in a law firm? Why?

51. I see your highest mark is in Criminal law. We don't practice Criminal law – will that not bother you?

52. Tell us about one of the deals our firm has been involved in.

53. How would your friends describe you?

54. Who would you like to be the next Prime Minister and why?

55. If you could be Mayor of London, what is the first thing you would change?

56. What are your three best (or worst) qualities?

- It is useful to think about questions like this before you are asked them – it can be difficult to think of 3 qualities on the spot.

- Use this opportunity to sell yourself to the firm and think of qualities they would be interested in. Saying your three best qualities are 'singing, dancing and baking' are not really conducive to a successful legal career. Avoid coming across as too arrogant.

- If you are asked for three of your worst qualities, think of things that could also be construed as positive qualities or at least are not serious 'bad' qualities. For example, admitting that you are a perfectionist and do not like delegating work because you trust your own attention to detail and thoroughness more, is really a good quality dressed up in disguise!

- Don't be afraid of using appropriate humour. Your final good/bad quality could be a bit light hearted. Remember, law firms are looking for interesting individuals, so it is important to convey your personality to them.

57. Describe a challenge you have faced. Why was it a challenge? How did you overcome it? What did you learn?

58. Would you prefer to be captain of the Second Team or a reserve in the First Team? Why?

- Like most of these questions, there is no right or wrong answer. The test is in how you think and your ability to justify your answer.

- For example, you might say you would prefer to be a reserve in the First Team because you would be motivated to work hard in the hope that you will eventually play on the First Team and would enjoy training alongside and learning from players who are more skilled than the Second Team players.

- Similarly, you might say you would prefer to be captain of the Second Team as you enjoy being in a position of leadership and are happy to motivate others around you, working to a common goal (of rising up in the league). You could say you would prefer to be part of a team, being actively involved in playing matches, rather than sitting around in the wings waiting to be moved off the reserve bench.

59. Describe a situation where you have encountered difficult people. How did you manage to persuade them to come round to your way of thinking?

60. If you could be another person, who would it be and why?

61. What is your proudest achievement? Why?

62. What do you do in your spare time?

63. What would be your ideal day?

64. If you could do any job in the world, what would it be?

- It would be tempting when asked this question to answer with an enthusiastic account of how you would be a Solicitor above anything else. Whilst this may be the case, for most us there is a dream job that does not entail pouring over the Companies Act for hours every day!

- So say you would be a sports star, musician, stunt man or astronaut and your reasons why. Try to make the answer as interesting as possible and give as much of an insight into your personality through your answer.

- (NB: Try to avoid saying that your dream job is something which is perfectly achievable. Your interviewers will wonder why you want to be a Solicitor if you have just told them that your dream job is being a primary school teacher!)

65. I see you were captain of your school hockey team? What did this position of responsibility entail?

66. If you could stand on a soap box in Hyde Park Corner, what would you shout about? Why?

67. What do you think is the most serious issue our country faces? Why?

68. What makes a good leader?

- Good Communication skills;
- Ability to be decisive when necessary;
- Understanding that different factors motivate different people;
- Being confident in your field of expertise and so respected by your team members;
- Willing to listen to different points of view/external factors;
- Good sense of humour; and
- An understanding of team-members' different strengths and weaknesses and how to best utilise each person's skills set.

69. Should we have gone to war with Iraq?

70. What do you think about global warming?

71. What do you think about the Congestion Zone? Do you think it works?

72. Are you a member of any societies? What role have you played in them?

73. Why do you think competition is important?

- Competition concerns amongst the major supermarkets in the UK have been a hot topic for some time. The Competition Commission has been investigating competition between Tesco, Sainsburys, Asda and Morrisons as they all seek to expand their number of branches nationwide.

- Competition is important for many reasons:

  - Provides the consumer with choice. We enjoy being able to choose which superstore we shop at and would resent being forced to spend all of our money in only one store.

  - Lowers prices of goods. If there was only one supermarket, it could set whatever prices it liked (and would obviously set them as high as possible). To win customers, supermarkets must drop their prices.

  - Provides a greater variety of goods and services to the consumer. The greater the competition, the more variety of products the supermarkets will try and offer to make them more attractive to the consumer.

  - Improved customer service. To win customers and their loyalty, supermarkets will be forced to give a friendly, helpful service.

  - Competition encourages innovation. Supermarkets will be forced to create new products and services and come up with new ideas to win customers.

74. Should we join the Euro? Why?

75. Imagine I am an alien who has just arrived on earth. Explain the stock market to me in simple terms.

76. What is your favourite film and why?

77. If you could be any fruit, what would it be and why?

- There is obviously no one right answer. Rather the interviewer is looking at your ability to reason and argue a point.

- For example, "I would choose to be a pineapple because, just like me...:

  - It has a unique appearance and makes a striking first impression!

  - It is a 'larger than life' fruit, not bland and does not fit into a 'one-size-fits all' box!

  - Whilst it may have a resilient, hard outer-shell, inside is a soft, sensitive centre, which is universally liked!

  - It is a versatile fruit and works well with other members of the fruit family!

78. What is your favourite book and why?

79. Should we abolish Royalty in our country?

In favour of the Monarchy:

- The Queen provides a figurehead for the nation - a good Head of State as opposed to a President?
- Royalty represents hundreds of years of tradition and defines part of the British culture.
- The Queen provides continuity through changing governments.
- The Queen has been praised by several Prime Ministers for providing good political advice on a variety of issues.

Against:

- Is it not controversial to have a non-democratically elected person as Head of State?
- The Monarchy perhaps represents aristocracy - can the population really identify with the members of the royal family?
- The Monarchy is nothing more than a convention within UK politics.
- Financial burden on the taxpayer in funding high security protection and international trips etc.

80. If you could have one superpower - what would it be any why?

81. If you could invite 5 people (dead or alive) to a dinner party, who would they be and why?

82. What do you think about fox hunting? Should it be banned or is it harming countryside communities?

83. Do you think lawyers are overpaid?

84. Why do you think the legal profession is important?

85. What 3 items would you take to a desert island? Why?

86. How many other firms have you applied to?

In our experience about 10-25 is the average number of applications each student makes. Your interviewers may be a little alarmed by anything that is under 3 or over 30, but any number is acceptable as long as you provide sound reasons for your answer. However, take care that you do not give the impression that each particular firm is merely another number in your 'scattergun' approach to finding a training contract (however true that may in fact be!)

87. Magic Circle firms pay more – why did not you apply to one of those?

88. Tell us about your journey here.

89. A-Levels are a lot easier than they were in my time - are standards dropping?

90. Why did you study Science in preference to English for your A-Levels? What use could Physics A-Level be to a lawyer?

91. Is Inheritance Tax ("IT") a fair thing? In the current economic climate most people owning houses in London will fall into the IT bracket. What would you do if you were Chancellor?

92. Will property prices crash in London?

93. Why did the Stock Market take such a hit last month?

94. Should we teach Chinese rather than French in schools?

95. Would bringing back National Conscription be a good thing?

96. What do you need to create a valid contract?

- An offer;
- Acceptance of the offer;
- Consideration;
- An intention to be legally bound; and
- Certainty.

97. What is pro-bono work? Why do we encourage it?

98. What newspapers do you read?

99. What is the biggest mistake you have made? How would you do things differently next time?

100. What is your opinion on the devolution of Scotland and Wales, is it a good thing?

101. How would you go about enforcing a contract that you were a party to?

102. What do you think is the most important area of law?

(There is no "correct" answer - just make sure you fully justify your points.)

- Contract? Probably the most important area as all other areas can be (and generally are) agreed upon and enforced by contract (e.g. contracts for the sale of land; IP transfers; compliance with environmental regulations etc.).

- Statute? Statute could in theory override any and all contractual agreements currently in existence.

- European law? Conflict between supremacy of EU law over UK Legislation.

- Human Rights? The relative value of contractual agreements versus fundamental human rights and freedoms.

103. If you were given £5,000 how would you promote yourself and the firm?

104. Give me an example of a time when you took a risk.

105. If you were managing a struggling football club, would you invest in better players or in better conferencing facilities to gain other forms of revenue?

106. Do you think a General Election should be held soon?

107. What has been your biggest regret and why?

108. What do you think about the European Constitution?

109. What do you think about the recent stock market turmoil in the States?

110. Who do you think will be the next President of the United States?

111. Should guns be banned in the United States?

112. What would you change about the UK tax system?

113. In light of your own schooling, where do you stand on the private school versus state school debate in the UK?

114. How do you think the 21st century will be defined?

115. What do you do at the weekends?

116. What do you think about the issues facing the UK concerning asylum and immigration?

Understand the difference between immigration and asylum seeking!

- Immigration is the relocation of a person to their non-home domicile for non-asylum reasons (e.g. seeking employment / relocation of family etc.). Note the current debate on immigration within the EU - working visa restrictions on Romanian immigrants in the UK (and reciprocal measures taken by the Romanian government in relation to UK employees).

- Asylum - genuine and non-genuine asylum seeking. Human rights debate. What about asylum seekers that commit criminal acts within the UK? Should the UK continue to accommodate genuine asylum seekers that are not willing to conform to UK law?

- Population increase concerns.

- Citizenship tests and language requirements? Should there be an English language requirement for immigrants?

117. What do you think about the NHS?

118. Do you think there are too many graduates in the UK?

119. Do you think pensions are a good thing?

120. In your opinion, should western countries wipe out 3rd world debt?

121. What do you think about the welfare state in the UK?

Consider some of the following:

- Distribution of wealth to those in need of financial support.

- Are welfare payments too high?

- Is it a disincentive to the unemployed to find employment?

- Helps those who cannot help themselves e.g. the disabled, the elderly, single parent families etc.

- Is it an unfair taxation on those who work hard and earn above a certain level of income? Is it unfair that those high earners have little or no say as to how that wealth is redistributed?

- Free healthcare ensures that everyone is looked after when needed and in turn enables them to return to employment more quickly.

- Abuse of the system? Is it only encouraging more people to depend on the state, punishing those individuals who work hard and pay taxes?

122. Should capital punishment be reintroduced in the UK? Why?

123. Do you believe children should be misled into thinking that fictional characters and myths (e.g. Father Christmas) are real?

124. Do you think religion should be taught in schools?

125. In your opinion, should cannabis be legalised?

126. Do you think ASBO's are effective?

127. How would you reduce your carbon footprint?

128. Is the proliferation of glossy celebrity magazines good or bad, why?

129. What do you think will be the impact for the future economy of such inflated house prices?

130. Do you think the British Government should be doing more to promote British farming?

131. Do you think obese patients should be denied treatment on the NHS?

132. If you could avoid one place in the world, where would it be and why?

133. Do you like Marmite?

134. Do you agree that the minimum school leaver's age should be 18?

Yes:

- Gives children the chance to mature before making important life decisions.
- Increases the skills base of the UK in relation to literacy and numeracy.
- Potential to combine further education with vocational apprenticeships.
- Keeps unemployment numbers down.

No:

- Non-academic children may not benefit.
- Extra cost to educate children for a further 2 years who may not be interested in learning.
- Lost tax revenues from 16-18 year old school leavers in employment.
- Preventing entrepreneurship in the young?

135. What personality trait do you deplore most in others?

136. What personality trait do you admire most in others?

137. Do you think British nationals should be given priority in jobs over non-British nationals in the UK?

138. If you could go anywhere in the world, where would you go and why?

139. Should public transport be free?

140. What is your opinion on cloning?

141. Should Turkey be allowed to join the EU?

In favour:

- In May 2004, ten countries were admitted to the EU and no referendum was held – why should Turkey be treated any differently?
- Many believe that Turkey has long been viewed as a European country.
- The EU should promote and welcome new cultures and social and economic structures.
- Promotes the concept of free trade and the free movement of workers across Europe. EU countries could benefit from additional employees coming from Turkey.

Against:

- The Turkish economy, political structure and culture do not fit easily into the EU model.

- If Turkey's GNP is less than the EU average, it may require cash injection to bring the industries, health care and infrastructure up to EU standards. The subsidies that the richer western countries pay could increase significantly as a result. This could be reflected in our own council tax, government spending and general hidden taxes.

- Turkey would have to accept EU legislation, much of which sits at odds with some of Turkey's religious laws.

- Raises border control and immigration issues.

142. How do you balance respecting an individual's human rights versus protecting the human rights of the general population?

143. What do you think about the detention of suspected terrorists?

144. Do you think trial by jury is effective?

In favour:

- Represents the views of a cross section of society rather than one white, male, middle-class judge.

- Provides an important check against state power.

- Involves members of the public, making the legal system appear accessible and relevant to all.

- Juries arguably provide a more unbiased and sympathetic hearing than a judge who may be tired of listening to the same offence being committed again and again.

Against:

- Each jury member is supposed to provide an independent viewpoint. In reality, jury members easily influence each other. More dominant members of the jury can persuade less dominant members to come around to their way of thinking.

- Jury members are not experts in the relevant legal subject and are often required to understand complex legal cases and evidence. Many jury members are not adequately qualified to do this. A single expert judge would be preferential.

- Juries are expensive, costing the taxpayer money in the provision of accommodation, transport and living expenses etc.

- Certain trials such as sex offending cases or murder trials can be traumatic to jury members who are forced to hear harrowing evidence.

- Elongated trials as juries try and come to a decision.

145. Should hereditary peerage be abolished?

146. What do you think of George Bush?

147. Should the current law protecting copyright for 50 years after the death of the author be extended?

148. Name 5 key factors that help make a successful business?

Some suggestions:

- A product that customers want.
- A strong management team with good leadership and motivational skills.
- A strong team of skilled and loyal workers.
- A creative, strategic business model.
- Perseverance in a volatile market - riding out the rough with the smooth.
- Remaining competitive in the market by keeping abreast of changes in the market and creating new, innovative products.
- Providing value for money products coupled with high quality customer service.
- Understanding your market, your competition and what your customers want.

149. During your training contract your dad, who is short of money comes to you and asks you to draw up a will for him quickly so he does not have to pay costly Solicitor's fees. What do you do?

150. Imagine you are the Chief Executive Officer of a Public Limited Company which is in financial difficulty. Two of your senior officers suggest conflicting business strategies, the first gives short-term gains and causes a rise in share prices immediately therefore relieving the pressure on you and the rest of the Board to resign. The second is a long term strategy, but of a higher risk. What strategy would you support and why?

151. Are we living in an Orwellian nightmare?

Some suggestions:

- The proliferation of surveillance cameras in towns and cities;
- Endless databases recording every transaction we make including credit card and bank details;
- Governmental influence on education (strict national curriculum guidelines) affecting what our children learn from a young age;
- Databases recording DNA and other evidence;

- Extensive police powers (of arrest, search, phone tapping etc.).

152. How should the UK promote its own sustainable energy sources?

153. Should torture ever be used in circumstances where it is of importance to national security to extract information from criminal suspects?

154. What do you think are viable alternatives to incarceration?

155. Do you agree with 24 hour drinking licences currently in place in the UK?

156. Do you think the sex offenders list should be made public?

157. Can you tell us what the LSE, AIM, FTSE 100, NYSE, Dow Jones and NASDAQ are?

- The **London Stock Exchange** (**LSE**) is a stock exchange located in London. As one of the largest stock exchanges in the world, it has many overseas listings as well as UK companies.

- The **Alternative Investment Market** (**AIM**) is a sub-market of the London Stock Exchange. It allows smaller companies to float shares with a more flexible regulatory system than is applicable to the main market.

- The **FTSE 100 Index** is a share index of the 100 most highly capitalised companies listed on the London Stock Exchange. FTSE is an abbreviation of 'Financial Times Stock Exchange'. The index is maintained by the FTSE Group, a now independent company which originated as a joint venture between the Financial Times and the London Stock Exchange. FTSE 100 companies represent about 80% of the market capitalization of the whole London Stock Exchange.

- **The NASDAQ** *(**N**ational **A**ssociation of **S**ecurities **D**ealers **A**utomated **Q**uotations system)* is an American stock market. It is owned and operated by The Nasdaq Stock Market, Inc. the stock of which was listed on its own stock exchange in 2002. NASDAQ is the largest electronic screen-based equity securities market in the United States. It has approximately 3,200 companies, lists more companies and on average trades more shares per day than any other U.S. market.

- **Dow Jones** - this is a market indicator (a method of measuring the stock market's performance). The Dow, created over 100 years ago, tracks the performance of 30 well established companies, often called 'blue chips' (there are actually over 12,000 public US companies, but the Dow only measures 30.)

- The **New York Stock Exchange** (**NYSE**) is nicknamed the "**Big Board**" and is a New York City-based stock exchange.

158. Should Heathrow be allowed to open a 3rd runway?

159. What do you think about the Enron scandal?

160. What do you think makes an effective negotiator?

- Good preparation. Knowing what points you will and will not concede on.
- Good communication skills.
- Setting lowest and highest bench marks - knowing the absolute minimum you will agree to and the maximum you hope to walk away with.
- Understanding what the other party wants and why.
- Predicting what the other party will ask for and how you will respond in advance.
- Offering to draft the documents. The other party will be forced to reply to your suggestions.
- Ensure time is on your side so that you do not concede points as a result of time pressure.
- Aim for a win-win situation. The best negotiations will be where both sides come away from the table feeling like they have 'won'.

161. What are your thoughts on genetic modification?

162. Do you agree with the proliferation of low cost air travel?

In favour:

- Generates billions of pounds in employment, tourism and manufacturing.
- Makes worldwide travel accessible to those who could not previously afford it.
- Promotes effective global business networks.
- Some argue that environmentalists attack aviation for emotive reasons. Arguably planes are less noisy and cause less pollution than they did 20 years ago. Money is constantly being invested to improve efficiency and the impact that planes have on the environment.

Against:

- Contributes to global warming.
- Air travel is the fastest growing source of climate-changing pollution in the UK.
- Encourages people to fly instead of using other more environmentally friendly methods of transport such as trains and buses.

163. What is the greatest invention of the 21st century?

164. Should police officers be armed with guns whilst on duty?

165. Is the internet a good or a bad thing?

166. Should people that pay private healthcare or private school fees be entitled to pay less tax?

167. Should corporal punishment be brought back into schools?

168. How should the government encourage more people to vote?

169. Do you agree with the "City LPC"? (Where a consortium of the larger firms insist their trainees attend a tailored LPC course provided exclusively to trainees at those firms.)

170. How do natural disasters impact on the financial markets?

171. Do you think large banks abuse their position of power?

172. Should larger law firms be obliged to undertake a certain amount of pro bono work?

173. Do you agree with the globalisation of large name brands in non-western societies?

174. Should the government do more to protect the sale of products made through the exploitation of 3rd world workers?

175. What do you think about the increasing popularity of social networking sites?

176. One of your closest trainee friends is boasting to a group of you in the pub about how he binned 20 property files before he left his seat in Real Estate. What do you do?

177. Whose responsibility is it to ensure fair trade over free trade?

178. Do you think the amount of money invested in the Olympics is justified?

- Provides a showcase for London as a global city.
- Benefits local areas and transport links - encouraging regeneration.
- Encourages foreign direct investment (bringing foreign investment to the UK).
- Encourages young people to engage in certain Olympic sports.
- Gives UK residents the chance to see the Olympics in the UK - a rare occurrence in one's lifetime.

179. Super-casinos - are they a good thing or a bad thing?

180. Should the state have a role to play in what is printed in newspapers?

181. Do you think the National Lottery is a good thing?

In favour:

- As a huge charity foundation it gives money to an extensive array of charities and promotes schools, sporting foundations and other social welfare organisations.
- Provides entertainment for family, friends and work colleagues.

Against:

- Instant wealth can create unhappiness with jackpot winners unable to cope with their new found wealth.
- Encourages gambling.
- Only a fraction of the ticket purchase price goes to charity.
- Frequently, those who buy tickets are the less affluent members of society who cannot afford the tickets and who are misguided as to their very low chances of winning the jackpot.

182. Why should we offer you a training contract?

183. Should women be allowed to fight on the front line?

184. Would you like to run your own law firm? If so why? If not, why not?

185. Do you think "proportional representation" is better than a "first past the post" system of voting?

186. What do you think will be the next big consumer "must have" item?

187. Is the BBC anti-competitive (as it has a monopoly over public funds)?

188. Should all public services be privatised?

189. How do you deal with stress?

190. If we were to offer you a training contract, how would you ensure you stood out as a good trainee during a training contract with us?

191. How do you think the legal profession could be improved?

192. What would you put into Room 101?

193. To what extent are party politics redundant?

194. Should we have a referendum for all major national decisions?

195. Should we implement a written constitution?

196. Should Partners be made to retire at a certain age?

In favour:

- Makes partnership status more achievable thereby motivating associates and junior lawyers to work hard to achieve this promotion.

- New and younger partners could create a more dynamic and energy-fuelled partnership with a management structure that junior lawyers feel they can better identify with.

- Creates a fresh turnover of lawyers.

Against:

- Partners have a great wealth of knowledge - the more senior they are, the more extensive that knowledge and this promotes high quality work within the firm, better client satisfaction and ultimately more revenue for the firm.

- Law firms should act in the best interests of their clients. As long as the client demands a particular partner's expertise, that partner should be allowed to continue working.

197. Do you agree with the introduction of top up fees for university students?

198. Who would you say are our main competitors?

199. Do you prefer working on your own or in a team?

200. If you were to expand our global network, where would you open an office next? [*Requires you to know where they already have offices and where the legal market is growing.*]

NB: **DO NOT WORRY!** The above questions and model answers have been written from several years of experience. Law firms will not necessarily expect an answer of the depth we have illustrated, on the spot. Your interviewers will just want to see that you know the issues involved and can provide a well-structured and eloquent answer. It is also unlikely you will ever be faced with a large number of difficult questions in the same interview, but it is always worth being prepared for any eventuality.

50 Questions you could ask at Interview

This list covers a wide variety of questions and topics[6]. We have put a * by our favourites!

1. How much responsibility can I expect as a trainee?

2. Can you tell me more about your training and development programme?

3. Retention rates are important to me as I regard joining [X firm] as a long term career choice. How many of your trainees are still with the firm 2 years after qualification?

4. I understand that you provide the opportunity to go on international/client secondments. Could you explain a little more about how this process works in practice and how trainees are selected for secondments?

5. Is every trainee that wishes to go on secondment, able to go? Are they guaranteed a place?

6. How is good communication and quality of work maintained between your international offices? How do you

[6] Not all questions will be relevant to all firms. For example, they will not be impressed if you ask about international secondments when they only have UK offices. Ensure your questions are relevant to the firms you are applying to.

ensure consistency in quality of work and lawyers on a global basis?

7. Do you think it is better to open increasing numbers of international offices, or is it better to work on a 'best-friends' basis[7]? If the latter, how are the standards of quality, communication and good relations between lawyers at 'best friend' firms ensured?

8. What opportunities are there to get involved in pro-bono work?

9. How are trainees appraised?

10. * What do you think distinguishes [X firm] from its competitors?

11. I've read about one of your recent high-profile deals, acting for [X firm] in relation to [x deal]. In reality, as a trainee, what kind of work would I do on such a large deal?

12. How are seats in departments allocated? How much choice will I have in where I wish to go during my training contract?

13. How much client contact/marketing opportunities can I expect to receive/get involved in?

---

[7] Some firms favour 'best friend' offices as an alternative to opening their own offices overseas. This is where a law firm uses an independent 'best friend' law firm, not part of its group, to gain overseas advice in that specific jurisdiction.

14. Did you both (*referring to the interviewers*) train at the firm? If you were in my position now, would you recommend this firm to me?

15. At [X firm], what is the likelihood of trainees seeing deals through from start to finish given the seat rotations that happen every 6 months (*or 4 months if it is a 6-seat system*)?

16. What kind of support network is there for trainees (such as word processing support, secretarial assistance, photocopying and paralegal support etc.)? Is this available to trainees and partners alike and on the same terms? [*A good firm should provide trainees with as much access to support services as other Solicitors in the firm. After all, trainees are working for partners, albeit sometimes indirectly.*]

17. In your opinion, which would be more beneficial to me from a training perspective: a client secondment or an international secondment to one of your overseas offices?

18. I understand that law firms require all fee earners to record time. How does this work in practice? Will I have target billable hours? If so, what are they?

19. Large law firms have a reputation for having a high proportion of Oxbridge partners. Do you favour Oxbridge over non-Oxbridge graduates?

20. Many law firms claim to have an open door policy - in reality is this true at [X firm]?

21. How approachable are your partners? If I have a question, who can I ask?

22. How do you select your supervisors? How senior do they tend to be? Are only partners allowed to be supervisors at your firm?

23. I understand that during my training contract I must complete the professional skills course ("PSC"). When is this undertaken at [X firm]?[8]

24. Does the firm support any extra-curricular activities such as sports teams or subsidised language lessons?

25. * [*CLIENT CARE:*] I am aware of the importance of fostering and maintaining long term client relationships. In such a competitive market, how does [X firm] ensure a high standard of client care?

26. * What do you think about the difference between those firms that offer the conventional 4 seat training contract compared to those firms that offer trainees 6/7 seats? Who do you think the 6 seat system benefits more?

- 6 seats = arguably provides a better overview of practice areas for the trainee;

- 4 seats = trainees arguably get more experience and responsibility in each seat and so provides that

---

[8] Some firms require their trainees to complete the PSC at the start of their training contracts to get it out of the way. Others require their trainees to complete the course during their training contracts.

particular department with a higher quality of work, albeit the trainee sees fewer departments.

27. [*For women:*] What is the ratio of male to female partners? Is this ratio increasing or decreasing in favour of women?

28. I am fully prepared for the long hours required of me as a trainee or Solicitor in a City practice, but to what extent is a healthy work/life balance encouraged at [X firm]?

29. Is there a culture of staying late, even if there is no urgent work to be done? Are trainees expected to wait until the last Solicitor/partner has left?

30. What is the ratio of partners to associates/trainees in a typical department within your firm?

31. What is the ratio of trainees to paralegals at the firm?

32. Is there an obvious hierarchy within the firm - do partners sit in 'Ivory Towers'?

33. * I am aware of the vital importance of Solicitors working within a team. How do you promote a good team culture within [X firm]?

34. Are there any plans for a merger with a US firm? If so, how would this affect the firm's excellent culture?

35. How would you describe the culture at [X firm]?

36. Are well established UK firms like [X firm] threatened by the increasing presence and permanence of US firms?

37. How do you think the legal market will develop in the future? At the moment there appears to be a structure of 5/6 big Magic Circle firms, mid-tier firms and specialist/niche practices. Do you think that the only way to succeed in the future is to be either one of the biggest law firms, or to have a very specialist niche practice? Do you think mid-sized firms will suffer?

38. Do you have a mentor/buddy system for trainees?

39. * Clients are increasingly demanding a seamless, global service. I understand sometimes law firms open offices for the sake of saying they have an office in a certain country, even if it isn't profitable. What is your opinion about this and how does [X firm] achieve a seamless, global service?

40. Due to the size of the firm and the highly specialist practice areas, do you think your Solicitors become too specialist too soon?[9]

41. What departments or practice areas might the firm close in the future?

42. What departments are you hoping to expand?

43. Can you give me examples of how the firm is responding to changes in the market?

---

[9] In the very large firms, there can be several sub-departments, even within the Corporate department alone. It is possible to elect to specialise in one of these very niche practice areas upon qualification.

44. What is the % turnover of staff in general, excluding partners?[10]

45. What practices have you put in place to support a work-life balance among your workforce? (E.g. remote working from home, flexible working etc.)

46. How do you promote employee diversity within the firm?

47. Is there a trainee representative or committee that acts as a voice for the trainee population?

48. Are trainees encouraged to participate in the recruitment process? If so, how?

49. How much are trainees involved in business development? (E.g. pitches, client entertainment, networking etc.)

50. How many partners did [X firm] make up this year?

---

[10] An indicator of more contented workplaces is a 13-15% turnover. This is the figure most firms aim for. A turnover of 25% or more could be concerning.

Presentation Tips

If the title of this page alone induces the onset of 'clammy hand syndrome' and severe palpitations, fear not... help is at hand. Most of us admit to a dislike for public speaking, but having to give a presentation is a common task that you will be faced with not only on an assessment day but throughout your career as a Solicitor as well. Take a deep breath, and follow our suggested tips...

Preparation

- **Practice and preparation are key**

  Familiarise yourself with the material so that you know exactly what you are going to cover and in what order. This will make you feel more confident.

Preparing your material

- **Structuring your speech**

  A structure will make it easier for your audience to follow what you are saying and will assist you in getting the main points across.

  - **Introduction.** Tell your audience, in brief, what you are going to talk about and the main points you will make.

- **Content.** Deliver the content in the same order as you described in the introduction. Allow and plan for pauses - it enables the points to sink in.

- **End.** Deliver a strong and succinct conclusion. Do not ramble on. Re-emphasise the key points you have made.

- **Slides – keep text to a minimum**

  No more than 5 bullet points per slide as a recommended guide (people will be reading the text and not listening to you). Make sure the font is large enough for your audience to read from a distance.

- **Pictures**

  Don't be afraid of inserting the odd picture or diagram on your slides. They will help to get your ideas across and engage your audience.

- **Handouts**

  These can help guide the audience and remind them of the key points. If the handout is detailed it may be best waiting until after the presentation before you hand it out (otherwise the audience will read the handout and not listen to what you are saying).

Giving your presentation

- **Dress well**

  Look professional but make sure you feel comfortable as well.

- **Greet your audience warmly and introduce yourself** (if no one else has).

- **Positioning**

  Think about how you are going to stand or if you are going to move around the stage. Where are you going to position your arms? There is no perfect stance, choose whatever feels natural and comfortable.

- **Do not hide!**

  Avoid using lecterns where possible and stand where your audience can see you.

- **Speak loudly, with confidence and SLOWLY!**

  In your mind you may be speaking naturally, but to the audience you are probably on fast forward. Make a conscious effort to slow your speech. If you deliver your speech with conviction, your audience is more likely to believe what you are saying.

- **Fluency**

  When you stop to pause, stop! Avoid the temptation to fill it with words such as 'Um, 'Er' and 'Like'.

- **Think before you speak and take pauses**

  If you ramble on for 20 minutes without a break, your audience will find it hard to follow.

- **Audience participation**

  This keeps them interested and makes it feel more like an interactive 'talk' rather than a lecture.

- **Add some relevant humour**

  This can help your audience identify with you. (Make sure it is appropriate humour that is unlikely to cause offence!)

- **Eye contact**

  If you can, talk directly to the audience and not to the floor. If it is simply too scary to look at the audience, pick a point at the back of the room and focus on that. If it is a big room, remember to look to the left and right as well.

- **Tell stories**

  If relevant. It helps to get your ideas across and

engages your audience.

- **Do not read from a script or slide**

  It is more personal if you talk directly to your audience. If you need your notes with you, use them purely as an 'aide memoir'.

- **Ignore mistakes**

  If you ignore them and move on, so will your audience - don't keep saying "sorry" or dwell on any errors.

- **Be prepared for interruptions and questions**

  View interruptions and questions in a positive light. It means your audience is interested. If you feel it will be disruptive to your presentation, request that questions be saved until the end.

- **Have a glass of water nearby**

And remember... It is natural to be nervous. People that say they feel no fear are probably lying.

Other Forms of Assessment

Although many employers use application forms and interviews as their sole recruitment strategy, more and more law firms are using other methods of assessment to differentiate between applicants. We have provided a brief summary of the main types below.

a) Group Tests

- Often designed to test your communication skills, problem solving and team working abilities.

- It is important to get the balance right here. Recruiters are looking for people who not only contribute to the discussion but are also willing to sit back and listen to the opinions of others.

- Be confident and articulate. It can be intimidating if there is a dominant member in the group who clearly loves the sound of their own voice. Rest assured this dominant member is likely to lose points for failing to listen to others. Just make sure you listen to what people are saying and when you have something to contribute, be confident and speak up.

- Make sure you contribute something - if you say nothing at all you are simply shooting yourself in the foot.

- The group will probably have to come to a joint decision at the end of a specified time frame. Time keeping is a skill in itself - have an eye on the clock and encourage your group to start coming to a decision before time runs out.

Example:

You have 20 minutes to conduct the planning for a new town named Traineeville. The council has given you enough funding to only build three buildings and you as a group must decide what these buildings should be.

You will each be given one of the following roles and building to support and must come up with arguments to persuade the others why you want your specific building to be constructed:

- Tina the teacher (**school**)
- Ron the Religious leader (**place of worship**)
- Donald the future Dean (**university**)
- Simon the owner of Saintsesco chain of supermarkets (**supermarket**)
- Paddy the personal fitness trainer (**sports centre**)
- Percy the policeman (**police station**)
- Frank the fireman (**fire station**)
- Lesley the pub landlord (**public house**)

- Sally the owner of Selfrodges (**fashionable department store**)

- Olga - 90 year old lady (**old people's home**).

You will have ten minutes to prepare arguments for your character and then you will sit around the council meeting table to have a discussion about which three buildings to build. At then end of the meeting, you must have come to a decision as a group about which three buildings will be awarded funding.

b) Case Studies

You may be presented with a case study (which could take the form of a business scenario or letter from a client requesting your advice, or more simply, an article lifted from the business section of a newspaper). However the case study is presented, it is probably designed to test your ability to problem solve, think laterally, digest large quantities of information, order and structure your thoughts, and communicate clearly.

You may be required to:

- Summarise the problem in a few sentences;

- Identify the key issues;

- Identify the key stakeholders (i.e. the people the problem affects);

- Offer sensible solutions to any issues;
- Answer questions related to the case study; and
- Discuss the wider implications arising from the case study.

It is likely that you will be given a finite amount of time to read the study (perhaps 5 - 10 minutes depending on its length). The case study may be given to you to read and prepare for before an interview or sometimes during the interview itself. You will then be asked about the case study in the interview or perhaps asked to write a letter of advice in response to the study.

Example:

Frank Wong owns a successful chain of supermarkets called Wong Foods across Asia.

He now wants to infiltrate the UK and potentially the European market as well. He needs some initial advice on the issues he might face in establishing his business over here, and so contacts you.

Key points:

Tip: It is often helpful to go through the major departments in a large law firm and structure your answer around how each one relates to the particular question.

Key Stakeholders: Shareholders (if any), external investors who may be willing to fund the venture, employees, the supermarket chains that will potentially be in direct competition with Wong Foods in the UK/Europe etc.

Issues:

1. **Workforce:**

How will Frank assemble a workforce? How long will this take? Employment contracts will need to be drafted taking into account employee rights under the various jurisdictions (e.g. minimum wage/holiday entitlement/relocation allowances/pensions & benefits etc.)

2. **Funding:**

How is the expansion going to be funded? E.g. existing capital from Frank's personal savings or existing capital from the Wong Foods business in Asia. Perhaps he will fund the venture by bank loans or equity (i.e. issuing shares in the new venture in return for cash). Perhaps he will use a combination of these options.)

3. **Corporate:**

Will Frank set up a new company in the UK/Europe for the purposes of this venture? If so, what type of company (limited/unlimited/public limited company etc.) and how many companies if any? Will he simply take over or merge with an existing supermarket chain?

4. **Tax/National Insurance**:

What is the most tax efficient way to structure the proposed deal? Could there be serious tax implications in establishing his business in the UK/Europe compared with Asia. Tax considerations may affect the way Frank proposes to ultimately structure his venture.

5. **Property**:

Will Frank buy or rent premises for the purposes of setting up stores? Are there environmental factors to consider or perhaps planning issues that could cause problems and delays?

6. **Intellectual Property:**

Will there be any trademark issues? Will Frank be able to use the "Wong Foods" mark in the UK/Europe? If not, he may have to create a new name and therefore establish a completely new brand.

7. **IT:**

Will Wong Foods (like Tesco) have its own website where

customers can order online and perhaps buy other related services (insurance, credit cards, mobile phones etc.). Frank will need to think about expanding this global internet network - how is he going to sell online in Europe? Are there data protection/confidentiality issues he should be aware of?

8. **Outsourcing/suppliers/delivery services**:

These will need to be researched, cost projections calculated, profit margins analysed etc.

9. **Competition**:

Will Frank need to seek clearance from national competition authorities? This could be an issue especially if he plans to merge with an existing supermarket (note recent and ongoing OFT and Commission investigations into competition amongst the main supermarkets in the UK- Tesco, Morrisons, Sainsburys and Asda). Competition clearance can take a long time. This could affect the timetable for the deal.

10. **Commercial**:

Large numbers of commercial agreements must be negotiated: supply contracts, distribution contracts, outsourcing agreements, leases, advertising contracts etc.

c) Psychometric Tests

- Typically last half an hour and contain around 30 questions.

- Various types exist but they are all generally designed to test your personality and aptitude for the job.

- Many people find the tests frustrating. Be reassured that they are generally only used as part of the assessment process.

- Ask your careers advisor for some example tests so you can practice and gain an idea of what the questions are like.

- It is common to feel pressed for time in such tests. Work quickly but accurately. Read every part of the question carefully and do not be tempted to skim-read. Check answers at the end if you have time.

- If you are running out of time, do not waste minutes on confusing questions, go to the next clear question and return to the confusing ones if you have time at the end.

d) Assessment Days/Centres

- Most often with a group of fellow applicants (c.10 - 20).

- Generally held at the firm's offices but could be held offsite.

- Ranging from half a day to a full day.

- You may meet with current trainees/associates and partners (frequently over lunch). Be careful - although it is only lunch, always assume that every part of the day is assessed (unless you are told otherwise). Lunch with other members of the firm may be used to observe your networking and social skills. Even during a tour of the offices, Human Resources ("HR") will frequently ask trainees to give feedback on who they liked and who they thought were unsuitable.

- Can be intensive and demanding. The day is likely to be heavily timetabled with tests to be undertaken under strict time limits. This is aimed at testing your time keeping and ability to work under stress.

- Be engaging, positive and enthusiastic.

- You may be tested in a range of ways e.g. case studies, preparing and giving presentations, group exercises, role plays, negotiation exercises, psychometric testing etc.

> Example:
>
> You have received the following irate letter of complaint from a high profile client who believes they have been receiving a sub-standard service from the firm. Write a letter in response to them on behalf of the firm.

Example:

While you were on a plane to Barbados, jetting off for your well deserved summer holiday, it crash landed on a remote island. Thankfully everyone on board survived but you must now decide where to set up camp on the island and everyone must stay together.

You will be split into two groups: Group A and Group B.

Group A must come up with reasons to argue and persuade why everyone should set up camp on the beach.

Group B must come up with reasons to argue and persuade why everyone should set up camp in the forest, inland and far away from the beach.

You will have 20 minutes to come up with your arguments in your group and then your group must give a 5 minute presentation on your arguments to the other team. After both teams have presented their arguments, you will all come together to discuss and debate your reasons and must finally come to a decision, as a group, about where you will finally camp.

e) Writing letters

As illustrated above, writing a letter is a common assessment tool. It is always worth reminding yourself of the basics:

Addressing the right person

- Dear Sir or Madam: (use if you don't know who you are writing to).
- Dear Mr, Mrs, Miss or Ms Jones: (use if you know who you are writing to).
- Use Ms for women unless asked to use Mrs or Miss.
- Dear John: (use if the person is a close business contact or friend).

Correct opening (some examples)

- Thank you for your letter of March 5 2007,
- In response to your email dated 9 July,

Closing remarks

- Please do not hesitate to contact me if you have any questions.
- I look forward to hearing from you shortly.

Finishing

- Yours faithfully, (If you do not know the name of the person you are writing to.)
- Yours sincerely, (If you know the name of the person you are writing to.)
- Kind regards, (If the person is a close business contact or friend.)

Example letter format:

Freddy Mercury
Head of Music - Queen Records Ltd.
21 Disc Street
London E2 1KJ

5 October 2007

Dear Mr Mercury,

In relation to our telephone conversation earlier today, please find enclosed a copy of my latest album 'Law Rocks'.

Please contact me again if you require further assistance.

Yours sincerely,

Robert Marley
Enc.

If at first you don't succeed...

TRY AGAIN!

Securing a training contract is extremely competitive and many people do not succeed first time around. This should not alarm you, but instead encourage you that it is still possible to be successful further down the line. As one wise man once said "the early bird catches the worm... but the second mouse gets the cheese". With this mantra in mind here are a few handy tips on how to overcome the rejection, bounce back and secure the training contract you always wanted.

1. Do not panic

Coping with rejection is difficult, particularly if you feel like all your peers are managing to breeze through the recruitment process without as much as a sleepless night. There will always be someone in your year at university who you overhear nonchalantly complaining to a large group of friends how agonising it is choosing between Clifford Chance, Allen & Overy and Freshfields, but you have to play your own game.

2. Ask for feedback

Most law firms are more than happy to give feedback following an interview. Although phoning up the firm that has just rejected you, is probably the last thing you feel like doing, it will prove invaluable receiving constructive criticism.

3. Remember there is no time limit

Law firms will look at prospective trainees from the age of 19-40. In fact, the average age of a trainee is about 25-27 so you have plenty of time to make applications in subsequent years if necessary.

4. Enhance your CV

It is worth considering what you can do to enhance your CV. As we have highlighted on pages 23 - 26, law firms are looking for a wide variety of skills and attributes. It is easy to expand your own achievements - enrol on a language course, join a sports team, go travelling or work in industry for a year.

5. Paralegal

Becoming a paralegal is a great way to gain experience and enhance your prospects of securing a training contract. In certain circumstances it can even help you reduce the length of your training contract, so it is definitely time well spent!

SECTION 4:

VACATION SCHEMES AND TRAINING CONTRACTS

Vacation Schemes

Do not be misled... unfortunately a 'vacation scheme' does not mean a 3-week all-inclusive holiday in the Maldives. They are, however, the best way to gain an insight into working as a Solicitor in a particular firm. Law firms look favourably on those candidates that have completed one so, if possible, get one or more under your belt before you apply for a training contract. If you are unable to secure a vacation scheme, try to attend some law firm open days.

When do they take place?

- This differs from firm to firm, but vacation schemes are held at Christmas, Easter and (most commonly) during the summer (June- August).

How long are they?

- Schemes can vary in length from 1- 4 weeks. Most larger firms operate 2 to 3 week schemes.

Will I get paid?

- At most large firms- YES! Usually about **£150-£275** a week.

What do they entail?

- Vacation schemes will be structured programmes where you will sit in one or two departments in the firm to gain an idea of what it is like to be a trainee in that firm. The scheme will probably include presentations, talks, workshops and social events. There are usually about 10-20 students on each vacation scheme. They are designed to give you a better perspective of what working in a law firm is like.

Joint applications for vacation schemes and training contracts

- The application form for a vacation scheme is usually the same or at least similar to the application form for a training contract. Most of the large law firms operate a policy whereby you can elect to apply for both vacation schemes and training contracts on the same form. Many firms will fill their places as soon as they start receiving good applications so make sure you apply as early as possible.

Are they any fun?

- Definitely! Remember that it is often more competitive to secure a vacation scheme than a training contract and you will usually have been selected following an interview/assessment day. The scheme is a two-way process. The firm will wish to make a good impression and you will be treated to the occasional social event in the evenings (be careful not to get too drunk at such social events and embarrass yourself - it will almost certainly get back to HR). Equally, the firm will use the opportunity to see what you are like over the two or three week period. Ensure you make a good impression! Try to get as involved as you can in firm life and ask as many questions as you can to try and gauge what the culture is like and whether you would be happy working there.

Will the firm automatically offer me a training contract after my vacation scheme?

- There is no guarantee of this. Whilst many firms recruit heavily from their vacation schemes, do not be lulled into a false sense of security. Your vacation scheme is usually followed by an interview for a training contract (sometimes this interview or 'informal chat' occurs during the vacation scheme itself) and you will still have to work hard to persuade the firm that you wish to work for them over all other firms.

If I am rejected for a vacation scheme, will I automatically be rejected when I apply for a training contract?

- Not necessarily, no. Whilst some firms do keep a database and will automatically reject those who have already been rejected for a vacation scheme; most firms realise how competitive it is to get a vacation scheme place and so will consider training contract applications afresh. It is worth checking with the individual firm what their policy is on this before you apply.

Non-Law Students

An extremely large proportion of trainees/Solicitors did not study law at degree level. In fact, in the larger firms, it is common for a trainee intake in any year to be made up of c. 50% law graduates and c. 50% non-law graduates. Firms actively recruit non-law graduates and welcome the broad variety of skills that different degrees have taught. Here is a brief outline of the main points non-law graduates should know...

Who can apply for a training contract?

- Anyone that is completing (or has already completed) an undergraduate degree in any discipline and who meets the requisite academic requirements.

When?

- Non-law graduates apply for vacation schemes and training contracts in the last year of their degree (compared to law students who apply in their penultimate year of university). See our timeline from page 169 onwards.

The GDL/CPE

- In order to qualify as a lawyer, non-law students must undertake the Graduate Diploma in Law ("GDL") (also known as the Common Professional Examination ("CPE")).

This course lasts one year and is done before undertaking the Legal Practice Course ("LPC") (see page 12) which all law and non-law graduates must complete. The GDL/CPE covers the 7 core topics of a law degree (constitutional and administrative law, EU law, criminal law, contract law, the law of tort, land law and the law of equity and trusts).

How much will I be expected to know?

- During interviews for vacation schemes and training contracts, unless you have already completed the GDL/CPE, non-law students will not be assessed on a comparative legal knowledge basis to law graduates (after all, you have not studied it yet!).

- However, firms will want to see that you have researched this career choice thoroughly and have some idea of what to expect. You may well have to justify why you want to be a Solicitor more fervently than those who have studied law at degree level and explain your reasons for your degree choice.

- You will still be expected to have good commercial awareness (see pages 63 - 66) so ensure you keep abreast of what is going on in the legal and business press. You will also be expected to have undertaken good, relevant work experience.

International Students

Many UK law firms, particularly the larger ones, are international in scope. Their trainee intakes can be extremely diverse and include a large percentage of students who have studied abroad. UK law firms are held in very high regard throughout the world and it is a great place to start your legal career.

How can I tell if my overseas qualifications meet the UK academic requirements?

- The best way to ensure this is to contact the law firms you are interested in directly (see our contacts list from page 173 onwards). They will be able to give you more detailed advice on whether you will meet the requisite standards.

Will I need a visa?

- Anyone who wishes to complete a training contract and practice in the UK will require a work permit (except UK nationals and their spouses; spouses of UK residents; EU citizens and their dependants and commonwealth nationals who have ancestral visas through a UK grandparent).
- However, if a firm offers you a training contract then visa requirements can usually be sorted out with the help of the firm. Check with the firm you are interested in to

ensure they will recruit trainees that require visas to work in the UK. You may find that smaller firms (and even some of the larger firms) will not accept applications from individuals who require work permits.

- Work permits can only be applied for by the UK-based law firm that wishes to employ you. You as an individual cannot make the application yourself. Note also that securing training contracts in the UK is extremely competitive. Completing the GDL/CPE and LPC does not guarantee you a training contract or the automatic grant of a work permit.

Should I declare on my application forms that I need a work permit?

- Whilst some firms specifically ask the question 'do you require a visa to work in the UK?' many firms do not. If the form does not mention the question, it is up to you whether or not you declare this information. Some students believe it is better not to declare it (if given the option) as it gives them a chance to meet with the firm, explain their individual circumstances and persuade them that they are ideal candidates. Other students believe it is better to declare that they require a visa from the offset as it saves them wasting time on firms that will not consider students requiring visas.

- We advise that you make a quick call to the relevant firm before you apply to them to check that they will consider applications from students requiring a work permit. It will prevent you from wasting time on firms that will not consider you and will instead allow you to focus your applications on those firms that will.

Academic qualifications in the UK

Typically, students in the UK complete the following examinations before applying for training contracts:

- **GCSEs**: completed at age 16. Students usually take between 7-11 GCSEs, each GCSE being in a different subject. Grades range from A* (highest) to G (lowest).
- **A-Levels**: completed at age 18. Students usually take 3 or 4 A-Levels in different subjects. Grades range from A (highest) to E (lowest). UCAS applies a points system to each grade (such that an A = 120 points, B = 100 points, C = 80 points, D = 60 points). Some law firms stipulate a minimum A-Level requirement of 320 points for potential applicants.
- **Undergraduate degrees**: These courses typically last 3 or 4 years. Common degrees include the L.L.B. (Bachelor of Letters of Law), B.A. (Bachelor of Arts), B.S.c. (Bachelor of Science) and B.Phil. (Bachelor of Philosophy). Courses are graded as follows (highest to lowest): First Class Honours (1st), Upper Second Class Honours (2:1), Lower Second Class Honours (2:2), and Third Class Honours (3rd). To obtain a 1st you would typically have to achieve 70% or more in your exams (60%+ for a 2:1 and 50%+ for a 3rd). Many law firms set a minimum academic requirement of a 1st or 2:1 for potential applicants.

Contact the law firms you are interested in directly if you are unsure as to how your academic qualifications translate under the UK system. They may also advise you as to what examination results you should include, and in how much detail, on your application form/CV.

What else do I need to know?

- Ensure that you have all of your main examination certificates in the UK (for degree level examinations and any relevant law courses you have undertaken). Many employers will request to see them before or after your interview.
- All the useful information contained within this guide is equally applicable to students who are not studying in the UK, but who wish to apply to a UK-based law firm.

Remember...

- Law firms are increasingly global in reach and actively seek to recruit trainees with an international background (it can be to your advantage!). They will welcome candidates who can speak other languages (in addition to fluent English, which is essential) as Solicitors are often required to work alongside lawyers in overseas offices and many of the firm's clients will be large, international corporations.

Your Training Contract: What to Expect

No prospective trainee should embark on a legal career without a rough idea of what to expect. Such an insight can be easily gained through a vacation scheme or other relevant work experience, but even then the reality of life as a trainee can be far removed from a two or three week stint on a vacation scheme (where you will probably be allowed to leave on time each day and will be wined and dined on the occasional evening out). To this end we have provided a quick summary of the main points you need to know.

Training Contracts

It is a Law Society requirement that training contracts last 2 years, however this can sometimes be reduced due to any time spent as a paralegal. During your 2 years you will visit different departments within the firm to gain a variety of experience. In larger firms you may be required to visit 4 - 7 different departments (often referred to as 'seats') but in smaller firms of Solicitors, the training may not be structured at all. Law Society requirements state that you must gain a mixture of contentious and non-contentious experience and additional internal training.

At larger firms, you may be able to spend some of your training contract abroad working for one of the firm's overseas offices. Alternatively you may be able to spend a seat working in-house for one of your firm's clients.

The Professional Skills Course (PSC)

This must be completed during your training contract. The course consists of 3 modules: finance and business skills, advocacy and client care. It aims to build on the knowledge you have acquired during the LPC. It is sometimes done 'off-site', for example at the College of Law or alternatively will be administered within the firm. Many firms choose to make their trainees complete the course at the beginning of their training contract, in order to get the requirements complete from the offset, while other firms spread out the requisite modules over the 2-year training contract.

- **Recording Time**

All fee-earners have to 'record time' during their working day and trainees are (unfortunately!) no exception. This is nothing to worry about, it just means that due to the volume of clients large law firms have and the necessity to provide fee-breakdowns you will be required to record (usually electronically) how much time you spend doing any one task. This will need to be accompanied by a short narrative briefly describing what the work was. It is amazing how quickly you get used to this system but it does require you to be organised so that chargeable time is not lost during the course of the day.

- **Supervisors**

During your training contract you will usually share an office with a supervisor. The level of experience of your supervisor will vary from seat to seat. Some firms only allow partners to act as supervisors (but in most firms you will find it is a mixture of partners and associates). Your supervisor (as the name suggests!) will assume responsibility for your time in their department. They will often give you the majority of your work/support and will be your first point of reference for questions.

- **Appraisals**

The appraisal system will vary from firm to firm, but broadly speaking you will usually have some form of appraisal at the end and, perhaps, midway through each of your seats in order to assess how well you have performed. They will most commonly consist of a meeting with your supervisor and an HR representative. Your supervisor will ask for feedback from those within the department that you have worked for and this will form the basis of the appraisal. These are useful in terms of highlighting your strengths and weaknesses and providing constructive criticisms on how to improve.

- **Support Staff**

As a trainee you will usually have a secretary (commonly shared with other fee-earners). This means that you can delegate a lot of administrative tasks to them. In the larger firms you will also have access to paralegals, professional support lawyers, copy room/post room staff, word-processing departments, library staff and IT support teams (life savers when you somehow manage to lose the 200 page document you have just been working on for the past 3 days!).

- **Will I automatically be offered a job at the end of my training contract?**

Completing a training contract at a certain firm does not guarantee that you will be offered a job upon qualification. Towards the end of your training contract, it is likely that your firm will ask you to apply to the departments you would be happy to qualify in to. You may be required to write a statement or sit an interview as part of this application process and then you may or may not be offered a job (depending on how you performed during your training contract and whether or not there is an opening in your chosen department). You will usually find out if you have been offered a job approximately three months before you qualify, leaving you sufficient time to search for alternative jobs if you have been unsuccessful.

- **Salary**

Salaries vary between firms. As a rough guide you could expect the following (but check with individual firms before you apply):

Type of firm	Trainee starting salary	Newly qualified salary
Large City firm	c. £30,000 - £35,000	c. £60,000 - £65,000
US firm	c. £35,000 - £45,000	c. £70,000 - £90,000

UK regional Firm	c. £18,000 - £25,000	c. £28,000 - £40,000

- **A day in the life of a trainee**

One of the selling points of a legal career is the variety of work undertaken. It is true that no two days are ever the same. Here is an example day in the life of a trainee:

9.00am - Arrive at my desk, turn on PC. While waiting for computer to load, chat to supervisor about the comedy film I saw last night. Check for new emails and voicemails. Deal with any urgent matters immediately.

9.20am – Consider tasks on 'to do' list and prioritise them.

9.30am – Divert from prioritised list to deal with an urgent piece of research on limitation periods for a partner who has requested an answer by lunchtime. Spend the morning researching in the library and online. Discuss findings with partner.

12.00pm - Attend a lunchtime talk on Client Care (free sandwiches!).

1.30pm - Grab a coffee and have an update meeting with the team (two associates, a partner and myself) involved in Project Orange (involving a merger of two companies). Discussion of the next steps going forward and allocation of tasks.

2.30pm - Back to my desk to check emails and eat cake (there is a birthday in the department).

2.45pm - Start research and preparation for a lunchtime talk I will be giving to the department on Professional and Legal Privilege. Begin creating slides for the presentation.

5.00pm - Give a guided tour of the building and chat to a potential trainee who has just had his interview for a training contract.

5.30pm - Sit in on a conference call with an associate and two lawyers calling from New York to discuss various time frames for another project (involving the acquisition of a construction company).

7.15pm - Final check of emails and head to local drinking hole to catch up with fellow trainees. Kebab on the way home.

KEY INFORMATION

Don't Miss It!
Timetable of Key Events

Month	Event
September	• Law degrees and postgraduate degrees commence. • GDL/CPE and LPC start.
October	• Start researching! Find out as much as possible about law firms and start thinking about training contracts and where you would like to apply. It is never too early, even if you have just started your course. • First round LPC applications for 2008 entry. • Applications for the part-time LPC should be made directly to the relevant institution (deadlines vary).
November	• Start applying for vacations schemes (Easter and summer). Many firms will fill their places as soon as they start receiving good applications so make sure you apply as early as possible. • First round GDL/CPE applications for 2008 entry.

	• Applications for the part-time GDL/CPE should be made direct to the relevant institution (deadlines vary). • Applications for some larger commercial firms open for 2010 training contracts. • Law fair season! Most universities and LPC and GDL/CPE institutions will hold one each year anytime from November to January. Useful for talking to people from the firm, asking questions and picking up free brochures and miscellaneous goods (Frisbees, bouncy balls and enough pens to last the course)!
December	• First round LPC applications for 2008 entry close (although institutions may consider applications until the course is full). • Christmas vacation schemes take place.
January	• UCAS applications for LLB Law degrees (for students applying from within the EU) should be made by mid-January (or much earlier i.e. by mid-October if applying to Oxford or Cambridge Universities). • Applications for many summer schemes start to close from this month onwards (varies between firms) so check deadlines!

February	• First round GDL/CPE applications for 2008 entry close (although institutions may consider applications until the course is full). • Second round LPC applications for 2008 entry open.
April	• Relax, it's Easter! While eating chocolate, start thinking about exam revision - law firms expect good marks for every year of university, not just your finals. • Easter vacation schemes take place.
May	• Since most larger law firms fill their training contract places two years in advance, this means (for law undergraduates) applying by **June/July** in the summer between your second and third year of university (if completing a three-year law degree). For non-law graduates you should apply for a training contract in your final year of university before you start the GDL/CPE. Smaller firms may only accept applications for training contracts one year in advance.

June	• Summer holidays! GDL/CPE, LPC and university courses end. • For students applying from non-EU countries, make your application for a law degree to UCAS before the end of this month. • For postgraduate courses, check deadlines with the providing institutions - they vary.
July	• Many deadlines occur for training contract applications for 2008/09/10 however check individual firm websites since deadlines will vary.

Law Firm Directory and Websites[11]

Details about law firms, how to apply to that law firm, more specific details about what they are looking for in applicants and deadlines for applying, can all be found on their respective websites.

A	
Addleshaw Goddard	**www.addleshawgoddard.com**
Allen & Overy	**www.allenovery.com**
Ashurst	**www.ashursts.com**
B	
Baker & McKenzie LLP	**www.bakernet.com**
Barlow Lyde & Gilbert	**www.blg.co.uk**
Beachcroft	**www.beachcroft.co.uk**
Berrymans Lace Mawer	**www.blm-law.com**
Berwin Leighton Paisner	**www.blplaw.com**
Bingham McCutchen LLP	**www.bingham.com**
Bircham Dyson Bell	**www.bdb-law.co.uk**
Bird & Bird	**www.twobirds.com**
Blake Lapthorn Tarlo Lyons	**www.bllaw.co.uk**
Brabners Chaffe Street	**www.brabnerschaffestreet.com**
Bristows	**www.bristows.com**
Burges Salmon	**www.burges-salmon.com**

[11] This list contains the larger law firms that have offices in the UK. Details of other law firms not listed can be found on The Law Society's website (www.lawsociety.org.uk).

C	
Charles Russell LLP	**www.cr-law.co.uk**
Clarke Willmott	**www.clarkewillmott.com**
Cleary Gottlieb Steen & Hamilton LLP	**www.cgsh.com**
Clifford Chance	**www.cliffordchance.com**
Clyde & Co	**www.clydeco.com**
CMS Cameron McKenna	**www.cms-cmck.com**
Covington & Burling	**www.cov.com**
D	
Dechert LLP	**www.dechert.com**
Denton Wilde Sapte LLP	**www.dentonwildesapte.com**
Dickinson Dees	**www.dickinson-dees.com**
DLA Piper	**www.dlapiper.com**
DMH Stallard	**www.dmhstallard.com**
Dundas Wilson	**www.dundas-wilson.com**
E	
Eversheds LLP	**www.eversheds.com**
F	
Farrer & Co	**www.farrer.co.uk**
Field Fisher Waterhouse LLP	**www.ffw.com**
Freshfields Bruckhaus Deringer	**www.freshfields.com**

H	
Halliwells	www.halliwells.co.uk
Herbert Smith	www.herbertsmith.com
Hill Dickinson LLP	www.hilldickinson.com
Holman Fenwick & Willan	www.hfw.com
Howes Percival	www.howespercival.co.uk
I	
Ince & Co	www.incelaw.com
Irwin Mitchell	www.irwinmitchell.com
J	
Jones Day	www.jonesday.com
K	
Kendall Freeman	www.kendallfreeman.com
K & L Gates	www.klgates.com
L	
Latham Watkins	www.lw.com
Lawrence Graham	www.lg-legal.com
Linklaters	www.linklaters.com
Lovells	www.lovells.com
M	
Macfarlanes	www.macfarlanes.com
Manches LLP	www.manches.com
Mayer Brown Rowe & Maw	www.mayerbrown.com
McGrigors LLP	www.mcgrigors.com
Mills & Reeve	www.mills-reeve.com
Mishcon De Reya	www.mishcon.co.uk
Morgan Cole	www.morgan-cole.com

N	
Nabarro	**www.nabarro.com**
Norton Rose	**www.nortonrose.com**
O	
Olswang	**www.olswang.com**
Osborne Clarke	**www.osborneclarke.com**
P	
Pannone	**www.pannone.com**
Penningtons Solicitors LLP	**www.penningtons.co.uk**
Pinsent Masons	**www.pinsentmasons.com**
R	
Reed Smith Richards Butler	**www.reedsmith.com**
Reynolds Porter Chamberlain	**www.rpc.co.uk**
S	
Shearman & Stirling LLP	**www.shearman.com**
Shoosmiths	**www.shoosmiths.com**
Sidley Austin	**www.sidley.com**
Simmons & Simmons	**www.simmons-simmons.com**
SJ Berwin	**www.sjberwin.com**
Slaughter and May	**www.slaughterandmay.com**
Speechly Bircham	**www.speechlys.com**
Stephenson Harwood	**www.shlegal.com**

T	
Taylor Wessing	**www.taylorwessing.com**
TLT Solicitors	**www.tltsolicitors.com**
Travers Smith	**www.traverssmith.com**
Trowers & Hamlins	**www.trowers.com**
W	
Weil, Gotshal & Manges	**www.weil.com**
WFW Global LLP	**www.wfw.com**
White & Case	**www.whitecase.com**
Withers LLP	**www.withersworld.com**
Wragge & Co	**www.wragge.com**

LPC Providers Directory and Websites[12]

University	Contact details	Full time	Part time
Aberystwyth University	Department of Law University of Wales Aberystwyth SY23 4NA Tel 0197 062 2735 Website www.aber.ac.uk	Y	
Anglia Ruskin University	Department of Law Bishop Hall Lane Chelmsford CM1 1SQ Or Department of Law East Road Cambridge CB1 1PT Tel 0124 549 3131 Website www.anglia.ac.uk	Y	Y

[12] To check for the latest accurate LPC information and contact details, visit The Law Society's website (www.lawsociety.org.uk).

Bournemouth University	The Business School Dorset House Talbot Campus Fern Barrow Poole BH12 5BB Tel 0120 252 4111 Website www.bournemouth.ac.uk	Y	
BPP's Law School, Holborn BPP College of Professional Studies, Waterloo	Holborn Campus 68-70 Red Lion Street London WC1R 4NY Tel 0207 430 2304 Website www.bpp.com/law Waterloo Campus 137 Stamford Street London SE1 9NN Tel 0845 678 6868	Y	Y
BPP's Law School, Leeds	Leeds Campus 2 Whitehall Quays Leeds LS1 4HG Tel 0845 678 6868 Website www.bpp.com/law	Y	Y

BPP's Law School, Manchester	Manchester Campus St James's Building 79 Oxford Street Manchester M1 6FQ Tel 0845 678 6868 Website www.bpp.com/law	Y	Y
Cardiff Law School	Law Building Museum Avenue Cardiff Wales CF10 3AT Tel 029 2087 6705 Website www.cf.ac.uk/claws	Y	
University of Central England in Birmingham	UCE Birmingham Perry Barr Birmingham B42 2SU Tel 0121 331 5595 Website www.uce.ac.uk	Y	Y
The College of Law, Birmingham	133 Great Hampton Street Birmingham B18 6AQ Tel 0800 015 9519 Website www.college-of-law.co.uk	Y	Y

The College of Law, Chester	Christleton Hall Christleton Chester CH3 7AB Tel 0800 068 0053 Website www.college-of-law.co.uk	Y	Y
The College of Law, Guildford	Braboeuf Manor Portsmouth Road Guildford Surrey GU3 1HA Website www.college-of-law.co.uk	Y	Y
The College of Law, London (Bloomsbury)	14 Store Street London WC1E 7DE Tel 0800 289 997 Website www.college-of-law.co.uk	Y	Y
The College of Law, London (Moorgate)	2 Bunhill Row London EC1Y 8HQ Tel 020 7291 1367 Website www.college-of-law.co.uk	Y	

The College of Law, York	Bishopthorpe Road York YO23 2GA Tel 0800 318 130 Website www.college-of-law.co.uk	Y	Y
De Montfort University	De Montfort Law School Office De Montfort University Leicester LE1 9BH Tel 0116 257 7177 Website www.dmu.ac.uk	Y	Y
University of Glamorgan	School of Law Pontypridd Mid-Glamorgan CF37 1DL Tel 0144 365 4450 Website www.glam.ac.uk	Y	Y
University of Hertfordshire	Faculty of Law St Albans Campus 7 Hatfield Road St Albans Herts AL1 3RS Tel 0170 728 4000 Website www.herts.ac.uk		Y

University of Huddersfield	Department of Law Queensgate Huddersfield HD1 3DH Tel 0148 442 2288 Website www.hud.ac.uk	Y	Y
Inns of Court School of Law	4 Gray's Inn Place Gray's Inn London WC1R 5DX Tel 020 7404 5787 Website www.city.ac.uk/icsl	Y	
University of Central Lancashire	Lancashire Law School Harris Building Corporation Street Preston PR1 2HE Tel 0177 220 1201 Website www.uclan.ac.uk	Y	Y
Leeds Metropolitan University	Leeds Law School Cavendish Hall Beckett Park Headingley Leeds LS6 3QS Tel 0113 812 3113 Website www.lmu.ac.uk	Y	Y

Liverpool John Moores University	School of Law Josephine Butler House 1 Myrtle Street Liverpool L7 7DN Tel 0151 231 3936 Website www.livjm.ac.uk	Y	Y
London Metropolitan University	Admissions Office 166-220 Holloway Road London N7 8DB Tel 020 7133 4202 Website www.londonmet.ac.uk	Y	Y
Manchester Metropolitan University	School of Law Sandra Burslem Building Lower Ormond Street Manchester M15 6HB Tel 0161 247 3046 Website www.mmu.ac.uk	Y	Y
Northumbria University	School of Law Sutherland Building Northumberland Road Newcastle-upon-Tyne NE1 8ST Tel 0191 227 4494 Website www.northumbria.ac.uk	Y	Y

Nottingham Law School	Belgrave Centre Chaucer Street Nottingham NG1 5LP Tel 0115 848 6871 Website www.ntu.ac.uk/nls	Y	Y
Oxford Institute of Legal Practice	King Charles House Parke End treet Oxford OX1 1JD Tel 0186 526 0000 Website www.oxilp.ac.uk	Y	Y
University of Plymouth	Marketing and Admissions Office Drake Circus Plymouth PL4 8AA Tel 0175 223 2864 Website www.plymouth.ac.uk	Y	
University of Sheffield	School of Law Sheffield S10 1FL Tel 0114 222 6770 Website www.shef.ac.uk	Y	

Staffordshire University	Law School Worcester College of Technology Deansway Worcester WR1 2JF Tel 0178 229 4452 Website www.staffs.ac.uk/schools/law	y	y
Swansea University	Department of Law Singleton Park Swansea SA2 8PP Tel 0179 220 5678 Website www.swan.ac.uk/law	y	
Thames Valley University	TC 320 St Mary's Road Ealing London W5 5RF Tel 0208 579 5000 Website www.tvu.ac.uk	y	

University of the West of England, Bristol	Faculty of Law Frenchay Campus Coldharbour Lane Bristol BS15 1QY Tel 0117 965 6261 Website www.uwe.ac.uk	Y	Y
University of Westminster	Admissions Office 4 Little Titchfield Street London W1W 7UW Tel 0207 911 5000 Website www.wmin.ac.uk	Y	Y
University of Wolverhampton	School of Legal Studies Arthur Storer Building Molineux Street Wolverhampton WV1 1SB Tel 0190 232 2222 Website www.wlv.ac.uk	Y	Y

GDL/CPE Providers Directory and Websites[13]

University	Contact details	Full time	Part time
Anglia Ruskin University	Anglia Law School Anglia Ruskin University Bishop Hall Lane Chelmsford Essex CM1 1SQ Tel: 0124 549 3131 Website www.anglia.ac.uk	Y	Y
University of Birmingham	Faculty of Law University of Birmingham Edgbaston Birmingham B15 2TT Tel: 0121 414 6289 Website www.bham.ac.uk		Y
University of Central England in Birmingham	School of Law University of Central England in Birmingham Franchise Street Perry Barr Birmingham	Y	Y

[13] To check for the latest accurate GDL/LPC information and contact details, visit The Law Society's website (www.lawsociety.org.uk).

	B42 2SU Tel: 0121 331 5595 Website www.uce.ac.uk		
Bournemouth University	School of Finance & Law Bournemouth University Talbot Campus Fern Barrow, Poole, Dorset BH12 5BB Tel 0120 296 5543 Website www.bournemouth.ac.uk	Y	Y
BPP's Law School, Holborn BPP College of Professional Studies, Waterloo	BPP Law School 137 Stamford Street Waterloo London SE1 9NN Tel: 0845 077 5566 Website www.bpp.com/law	Y	Y
BPP's Law School, Leeds	See above Website www.bpp.com/law	Y	Y
BPP's Law School, Manchester	See above Website www.bpp.com/law	Y	Y

University of Brighton	University of Brighton Brighton Business School Mithras House Lewes Road Brighton BN2 4AT Tel: 0127 360 0900 Website www.brighton.ac.uk		Y
University of the West of England, Bristol	Faculty of Law University of the West of England, Bristol, Frenchay Campus Coldharbour Lane Bristol BS16 1QY Tel: 0117 965 6261 Website www.uwe.ac.uk	Y	Y
Brunel University	Law Department Brunel University Uxbridge Middlesex UB8 3PH Tel: 0189 527 4000 Website www.brunel.ac.uk	Y	

<table>
<tr><td>City University</td><td>Department of Law
City University
Northampton Square
London EC1V 0HB
Tel: 0207 040 5060

Website www.city.ac.uk</td><td>Y</td><td></td></tr>
<tr><td>The College of Law (branches at Birmingham, Chester, Guildford, London and York)</td><td>The Admissions Department
The College of Law
Braboeuf Manor
St Catherines
Portsmouth Road
Guildford, Surrey GU13 1HA
Tel: 0800 328 0153

Website
www.college-of-law.co.uk</td><td>Y</td><td>Y</td></tr>
<tr><td>De Montfort University</td><td>School of Law
De Montfort University
The Gateway
Leicester LE1 9BH
Tel: 0116 257 7458

Website www.dmu.ac.uk</td><td>Y</td><td>Y</td></tr>
</table>

University of East Anglia	School of Law University of East Anglia Norwich NR4 7TJ Tel 0160 359 2520 Website www.uea.ac.uk		
University of Glamorgan	School of Law University of Glamorgan Pontypridd Mid-Glamorgan CF37 1DL Tel 0144 365 4450 Website www.glam.ac.uk	Y	Y
University of Hertfordshire	Faculty of Law St Albans Campus 7 Hatfield Road St Albans Herts AL1 3RS Tel 0170 728 4000 Website www.herts.ac.uk	Y	Y
Holborn College	Flexible Learning Holborn College Woolwich Road, Charlton London SE7 8LN Tel: 0208 317 6039 Website www.holborncollege.ac.uk		Y

University of Huddersfield	Department of Law University of Huddersfield Queensgate Huddersfield HD1 3DH Tel 0148 442 2288 Website www.hud.ac.uk	Y	Y
Keele University	Department of Law Keele University Keele Staffs ST5 5BG Tel: 0178 258 3229 Website www.keele.ac.uk	Y	Y
Kingston University	Kingston Law School Kingston University Kingston Hill Kingston upon Thames Surrey KT2 7LB Tel: 0208 547 7053 Website www.king.ac.uk	Y	Y
University of Central Lancashire	Lancashire Law School Harris Building Corporation Street Preston PR1 2HE Tel 0177 220 1201 Website www.uclan.ac.uk	Y	Y

Leeds Metropolitan University	Leeds Law School Leeds Metropolitan University Cavendish Hall Beckett Park Headingley Leeds LS6 3QS Tel 0113 812 3113 Website www.lmu.ac.uk	Y	
University of Lincoln	Enquiry Centre University of Lincoln Brayford Pool Lincoln LN6 7TS Tel: 0152 288 2000 Website www.lincoln.ac.uk	Y	
London Metropolitan University	Admissions Office 166-220 Holloway Road London N7 8DB Tel 020 7133 4202 Website www.londonmet.ac.uk	Y	Y

London South Bank University	Admissions Office South Bank University 103 Borough Road London SE1 0AA Tel: 020 7815 5725 Website www.lsbu.ac.uk	Y	Y
Manchester Metropolitan University	School of Law Manchester Metropolitan University Sandra Burslem Building Lower Ormond Street Manchester M15 6HB Tel 0161 247 3046 Website www.mmu.ac.uk	Y	Y
Middlesex University	Admissions Office Middlesex University The Burroughs Hendon London NW4 4BT Tel: 0208 411 5555 Website www.mdx.ac.uk	Y	Y

Northumbria University	School of Law Northumbria University Sutherland Building Northumberland Road Newcastle-upon-Tyne NE1 8ST Tel 0191 227 4494 Website www.northumbria.ac.uk	Y	Y
Nottingham at Kaplan Law School	See below for address details Website www.kaplanlawschool.org.uk	Y	
Nottingham Trent University	GDL Full Time: Nottingham Law School Belgrave Centre Chaucer Street Nottingham NG1 5LP Tel: 0115 848 6871 Website www.ntu.ac.uk/nls GDL part-time distance learning: Distance Learning Office Department of Academic Legal Studies Burton Street Nottingham NG1 4BU Tel: 0115 848 4271	Y	Y

Oxford Brookes University	Law Department School of Social Sciences & Law Headington Hill Hall Headington Oxford OX3 0BP Tel: 0186 548 4901 Website www.brookes.ac.uk	Y	Y
University of Plymouth	Admissions Office Drake Circus Plymouth PL4 8AA Tel 0175 223 2864 Website www.plymouth.ac.uk	Y	
Southampton Solent University	East Park Terrace Southampton SO14 0YN Tel: 0238 031 9501 Website www.solent.ac.uk	Y	Y
Staffordshire University	Law School Leek Road Stoke-on-Trent Staffs ST4 2DF Tel: 0178 229 4452 Website www.business.staffs.ac.uk/law	Y	Y

Staffordshire University and Worcester College of Technology at Worcester	Law School Worcester College of Technology Deansway Worcester WR1 2JF Tel: 0190 572 5555 Website www.wortech.ac.uk		Y
University of Sussex	Postgraduate Office University of Sussex Sussex House Falmer Brighton BN1 9QQ Tel: 0127 387 7888 Website www.sussex.ac.uk	Y	
Swansea University	Department of Law University of Wales, Swansea Singleton Park Swansea SA2 8PP Tel: 0179 220 5678 Website www.swansea.ac.uk	Y	

Thames Valley University	Thames Valley University TC 320 St Mary's Road Ealing London W5 5RF Tel 0208 579 5000 Website www.tvu.ac.uk	Y	Y
University of Westminster	Admissions Office University of Westminster 4 Little Titchfield Street London W1W 7UW Tel 0207 911 5000 Website www.wmin.ac.uk	Y	Y
University of Wolverhampton	School of Legal Studies University of Wolverhampton Arthur Storer Building Molineux Street Wolverhampton WV1 1SB Tel 0190 232 2222 Website www.wlv.ac.uk	Y	Y

NOTES